My Account

My Account

COLEEN ROONEY

MICHAEL  JOSEPH

PENGUIN MICHAEL JOSEPH

UK | USA | Canada | Ireland | Australia
India | New Zealand | South Africa

Penguin Michael Joseph is part of the Penguin Random House group of companies
whose addresses can be found at global.penguinrandomhouse.com

First published 2023
001

All photos in the inset © Coleen Rooney, except: p.4, bottom right: Jeans for Genes®©. For more
information please visit jeansforgenes.org; p.5, bottom left & right: Andy Stenning / Daily Mirror via
Mirrorpix; p.7, top left: Tony Ward & Abi Wyles / OK! MAGAZINE via Mirrorpix; p.10, top left: Max
Mumby / Indigo via Getty Images Europe; p.10, top right: Phil Rees / Alamy Stock Photo; p.13, top left:
Eamonn M. McCormack / Stringer via Getty Images Europe; p.13, top right & bottom left: Anadolu Agency /
Anadolu via Getty Images Europe; p.13, bottom right: Wiktor Szymanowicz / Alamy Stock Photo; p.14
top left: Karwai Tang / WireImage via Getty Images Europe; p.15, top left: Robert Wyatt / Vogue via
Condé Nast Britain ©; p.15, bottom centre: Alec Maxwell / Vogue via Condé Nast Britain ©

Set in 13.5/17.5pt Garamond MT Std
Typeset by Jouve (UK), Milton Keynes
Printed and bound in Great Britain by Clays Ltd, Elcograf S.p.A.

The authorized representative in the EEA is Penguin Random House Ireland,
Morrison Chambers, 32 Nassau Street, Dublin D02 YH68

A CIP catalogue record for this book is available from the British Library

HARDBACK ISBN: 978–0–241–67326–3
TRADE PAPERBACK ISBN: 978–0–241–67327–0

www.greenpenguin.co.uk

This book is for my boys.

Kai, Klay, Kit & Cass Rooney.
Ups and downs are natural in life.
Enjoy the good times,
battle through the hard times.
Always be true to yourself, as well as others.
Have respect, remember your manners,
be kind and most of all be happy!

I love you SO much.
I am proud of you and will always be here for you.
Let's enjoy our life together.

Love your Mum
xxxx

Wayne

I loved you then and I love you now x

Prologue

As far as being in the public eye goes, it was the biggest thing that had ever happened to me, and like nothing I'd ever experienced. My legal battle with Rebekah Vardy, and all that led up to it, was nothing to do with football or being the partner of a high-profile player. It was nothing to do with what I was wearing or where I was going. It wasn't about Wayne triumphing on the pitch or our relationship, or our family life. This was me, Coleen, centre stage in the spotlight. It was something scandalous and, ultimately, entirely out of my control.

The whole thing started small. Well, that's how it felt anyway. It meant something to me, because someone was abusing my trust, and that's why I did what I did. I just never expected it to mean so much to so many others. Looking back on the legal battle, it still amazes me how inflated it all got, how ridiculous, how serious. In the grand scheme of things, with all that's happening in the world, it really shouldn't have and needn't have. That's why I need to tell what happened in full, and that's not something I feel I can do in a magazine interview or a ten-minute slot on a chat show. I'd like to express my feelings about it and tell my side of the story from beginning to end, then draw a line under it and get on with the rest of my life.

For a long time, I've had both a personal and a public Instagram account. There are some things I like to share with close friends and family but don't necessarily want in the public domain. It's not that I'm trying to hide anything; most of what gets posted on my private account is just usual family stuff that any mum with kids might post. Sometimes there's a crossover, and I'll post the same thing on both accounts, but there are a few things that I prefer to keep to a close-knit group.

I get a lot of friend requests on my personal account, so many that I don't even have time to go through them. If someone I know pops up or we have friends in common, I'll have a look, and if I know them personally, I'll add them.

In 2017, during an extended stay at Mum and Dad's, while I was going through a particularly difficult time with Wayne, I took a photograph of me and two of my kids, who'd climbed into my bed. It happened all the time with my boys; they'd start off in their own bed at night but end up in ours by the morning. I posted the picture on my private Instagram account with a caption that said, *'Everywhere I go, the children always follow. I hope this lasts forever.'* Going through such a rough patch, I suppose I was just trying to say that as long as I've got the kids with me, I'll be fine.

As soon as the post went out, I started getting messages and comments from concerned friends who'd seen it. *'Are you alright?' 'I hope you're OK, Coleen.'* They were coming at me from all quarters.

Everyone knew what was going on, so I guess I shouldn't have been surprised at the outpouring, but the thought of going through and replying to all those messages felt overwhelming, so instead, I deleted the post. A day or so after, there was an article in the *Sun* about the post on my private Instagram – the one with the picture of the kids and me lying in bed together. This was something from my personal account reported in the press, which felt a bit strange. It wasn't something I was going to dwell on. To be honest, I already had enough to deal with, but it did cross my mind that someone I considered a friend, or at least trusted, might have leaked something to a national newspaper.

With everything that was going on then, I let it go, but a few weeks later it happened again, which unnerved me. By this time, I'd returned to the family home. Wayne and I hadn't worked through all our problems, but we were in the process of trying and at least talking things through.

Wayne and I are both patrons of the Alder Hey Children's Hospital in Liverpool, and every year Matalan make matching pyjamas for the whole family in aid of the charity. Each year, we post a photo of us all together, wearing the pyjamas, but given the fragile situation between Wayne and me, I decided only to post one of me with the boys on my public social media. I did take a shot of Wayne and the boys, but I decided to post that on my private account rather than the public one. This was a conscious decision because people knew we were having problems. The last thing I wanted was a barrage of comments and speculation about us being back together, all sweetness and light, while I was still trying to work things out in my own head and sort out my relationship with my husband.

A few days later, again in the *Sun*, there was a headline, 'Look Roos Back – Wayne Rooney is back at home – and in bed with Coleen – as she shares snaps with pals celebrating Halloween together.' The article referenced the picture I'd posted of Wayne and the children then talked about how I'd forgiven Wayne and just wanted to forget what had happened and move on. This was all peppered with comments and quotes from so-called 'insiders' – an entire story based on something I'd posted on my private account.

Something wasn't right. Was somebody I trusted passing on stories to the media? I had around 300 followers on my private account, so I decided to scroll through all of them to see if anyone jumped out at me – someone who might be inclined or have a reason to do something like that. My search didn't throw anything up. I couldn't immediately see anyone I thought might do something like that. After that, I started to wonder if someone might be doing it for money or had some kind of connection with the press. It made me feel unsettled and paranoid. I hated thinking about my friends in that way, and the last thing I wanted to do was accuse innocent people of going behind my back or betraying my trust.

In the end, I decided to put a post on my private page; a warning shot, I suppose you could call it. I took a screenshot of the pyjamas article with the caption, *'The grass strikes again. I put that picture on, wondering if it would appear in that horrible newspaper. You're accepted as one of my friends, if you really need the money that bad you could've always just asked instead of being sly.'*

Rebekah Vardy commented on the post, *'What a joke'* with an angry face emoji, then she messaged me on WhatsApp, and there was an exchange between us.

Becky: O M G W T F is wrong with people! Why have they taken that one of you and the kids and not of Wayne in bed! That would've been an even better story in their eyes dick heads! Hope you are okay x

Coleen: Sorry love, just getting back to everyone ... been up the wall since I got back from holiday and it was Kai's birthday yesterday. It was that picture of Wayne and the kids they gave to the Sun. However, they can't print it so they have just wrote about it. It's not even the photos am bothered about cause I have nothing to hide, it's just annoying that someone talking and sharing it with them!! Nothing I've ever dealt with before, but just thought I'd let them know I know what they are up to. Hope you're all OK, we're fine thanks, back to reality. Take care xxx

Becky: That is so bad! And the Sun of all people as well! Have you been through all your followers? No one with any celeb mag links? What about being hacked? I would be chomping if that was me!. Not on at all. x

Coleen: Yeh, been through all but can't remember anyone. Got a few people onto it trying to source but if they're getting the info they're not going to tell. Had things like this in the past and never got to find out x

Becky: Yeah, that's true! You don't think the paper has hacked your account do you? x

Coleen: No, very much doubt it. x

I didn't think much else about it at the time. I received a fair few concerned and sympathetic messages from friends after the post went up. The fact that it involved the *Sun* newspaper made it worse for many of them, given the paper's history with the people of Liverpool after Hillsborough. The problem with sharing the warning post was that it unsettled some people close to me.

'You wouldn't think I've done it, would you?' one friend asked me.

'I'd never do something like that, Coleen; I hope you know that,' someone else said.

These were people I'd never in a million years have suspected, and hearing them ask me made me feel awful. I hated the idea of someone feeling down, upset or worried because of something I've done or said. I try never to say something unless I know it to be accurate and true or I'm sure it's the right time to say it. In fact, I tend to hold things in, even if something's bothering me, rather than burdening someone else. I like to be sure of the facts.

If Wayne and I discuss or plan something big or exciting involving the children, he'll often tell them beforehand, so I'll step in.

'Don't tell them what we might be doing when it might not happen. You're getting their hopes up, and it might not come to anything.'

As I've said, I hate the thought of letting someone down and of somebody feeling uneasy because of something I've done or said. At the same time, I hated the idea that I'd let someone into my private space who'd betrayed my trust. Anyone I'd given my private Instagram account details to knows precisely why I keep it separate from my public one, so why would they do such a thing? It wasn't even that the stuff being leaked was anything of vital importance or something I'd be upset or distressed by; it was that I'd uploaded it to what I thought was a private platform. That was what bugged me the most. Still, I figured whoever the guilty party was would have seen my warning shot, so hopefully, that would be the end of it.

There was a lot happening all at once, but apart from being pregnant with our fourth child, none of it was good: the difficulties in my marriage, my personal stories being leaked. It all felt very stressful, but I somehow put my head down and carried on. When you have kids, that's all you can do. Sure, I had my down days, but they were nothing compared to the storm that was coming.

Before I get to the storm, I think I need to explain myself, or at least explain why I did what I did in the way that I did it. To do that, I have to tell you about the values my mum and dad instilled in my brothers and me as kids – honesty, fairness, kindness. I have to tell you how hard I've tried to hold on to them while growing up so very publicly, because that's all such a big part of it.

I have to go back to the start . . .

Chapter One

By the time baby Coleen McLoughlin arrived at the Oxford Street Hospital, Liverpool, on Thursday, 3 April 1986, Mum and Dad had been trying to have a baby for seven years. In fact, Mum had been having fertility treatment for so long that, at one point, she thought she'd never have children – so I was a happy surprise. For this reason, I've always felt loved and wanted, knowing the extended family was over the moon at my arrival.

My mum, Colette, was a nursery nurse who loved kids. The youngest of eight children, she'd married my dad Tony at eighteen – he was the middle one of five – so they'd both grown up in big families and wanted that for themselves. Mum had lost her mother, my nan, when she was just sixteen, so she had to grow up fast. Hearing her talk about it always makes me feel lucky to have had my mum there for me. It's something she never had, which is another reason being a parent was so important to her. As the youngest in such a big family, she'd missed out on precious time with her own mother as she grew into a young woman.

I was born in Liverpool, and we lived in Garston, where all my dad's family came from. Dad was a bricklayer, working for the Liverpool Corporation, and sometimes helped out with my uncle's building firm at weekends, and after Mum had kids, she didn't go back to work, preferring to be a stay-at-home mum. That was the way our house worked.

When I was about four, they nearly lost me after I caught chicken pox. Not unusual for a young kid, but unfortunately, the infection spread to my brain, causing encephalitis, where the immune system attacks the brain, causing it to become inflamed. At first, the doctor thought I was dehydrated and told her not to worry, but Mum knew something wasn't right. With things going from bad to worse, she took me to the hospital, where I ended up in intensive care. Of course, I don't remember that much about it, but for a while, it was touch and go if I would survive. The infection affected me so severely that I had to learn to walk all over again and regain my coordination. Mum tells me that my dad and various extended family members were at church praying for me to pull through.

I always liked school; I was a bright, bubbly kid with lots of friends. I was a leader and a planner within my group of friends – Mum says I was 'a bossy bitch', and she was probably right. I was an incredibly organised child who was happiest when things went my way – I wasn't a spoilt brat or anything; I just had a particular way of doing things.

Every New Year's Eve was spent at Auntie Maureen and Uncle Frankie's – my mum's sister and her husband – and I'd take it upon myself to put on some sort of production with my brothers and cousins. It was always the same. I'd spend ages planning it all out and then directing it with a rod of iron, but by the time it came to our big performance in the living room, I'd end up doing every part because I'd decided they weren't doing it right. And this is not just some distant, diluted memory either; there's documented evidence of my high-handedness in many an old family VHS. I had reason to watch one recently while making a documentary for Disney+, and oh my, was I bossy? I was clearly striving for perfection, and if I felt my brothers and cousins weren't up to scratch, I'd have to do it myself. That said, I don't think I was a naughty or selfish child. Mum tells me I had a bit of back-chat and always liked to have the last word, but that was about it. I wasn't a hellraiser and didn't cause them a lot of grief, which is probably a good thing, given how full their hands were. I reckon I just had a bit too much to say for myself, and most of the time, I made sure it never went unsaid.

I was the same all through school. I worked hard because I wanted to excel as much as I could. I wasn't naturally clever or overly academic, so I knew I'd have to work hard and revise to get the grades I needed, and that's what

I did. I put the work in and, consequently, my report cards were never a disappointment and I managed to stay up in the top sets for most subjects.

I enjoyed drama very much, and although I was a permanent fixture in all the school productions, I never got a leading part. The reason? Well, we always did musicals, and I couldn't sing, so I'd usually end up with the best non-singing parts up for grabs. For instance, in *Grease*, I was a T-Bird, and in *Bugsy Malone*, I was Fat Sam. I always did dancing and drama outside of school while my younger brothers, Joe, two years younger than me, and Anthony, three years younger, played football. We weren't spoiled, but Mum and Dad did their best to make sure we could pursue and enjoy the things we loved. We might not have been well off, but we never wanted for anything. We never went hungry either, although we weren't always thrilled about our parents' choice of sustenance.

Dad had boxed from a young age, so got in the habit of sticking to a healthy diet. It wasn't anything extreme, just what he saw as well balanced, but we all ate the same thing on a particular day of the week – every week. The menu was written on paper and stuck on the larder door, so we all knew what was coming. For example, Monday might be scrambled eggs for breakfast and chicken for dinner. Tuesday would be something completely different for all three meals but, as a family, we all ate the same. Wednesdays it was liver which, as kids, we hated. I managed to get through mine when I had to by drowning it in mint sauce, but that's what we got, and back then, it was a case of 'eat what you're given'.

I had a friend, Kelly, whose mum Debbie was friends with my mum. Sometimes, on a Wednesday, Debbie would ask me, 'You coming to ours for your tea tonight, Coleen? I'm doing spaghetti bolognese.'

'Oh yeah, please ask my mum if I can come to yours tonight, will you?'

She knew I hated liver night, and this was the only way to avoid it.

A bowl of baked beans with a slice of brown toast was another of my least favourite meals; that was our Wednesday breakfast, and not the best start to the day. Joe and I used to scoop spoonfuls of beans into Anthony's bowl when he wasn't paying attention. Friday, of course, was always fish – Mum would do cod in parsley sauce or something similar.

As regimented as it might seem, I'm grateful to have had parents who cared about our diet and well-being. We weren't eating takeaways and ready meals the whole time, and it taught me to have a healthy outlook on food from a very early age – although it probably took me a while to get the balance exactly right.

While I was doing my GCSEs, my friend Louise, who was a year older than me, was doing her AS-level exams. She'd come to ours for lunch during exam break because I lived just around the corner from the school. By then, I was getting my own lunches. I remember her looking at my chosen menu one day with a mix of fascination and horror – a bit of cod in parsley sauce, half a Mars bar and a Lucozade.

'What? It's brain food!' I told her. 'Feeds your brain!'

I was clearly inspired by my dad.

Back when we were little, though, Thursday was the best day because that was a chippy day, and it said so on the larder door! Dad would take us swimming in the evening while Mum watched on from the sidelines. She'd always pack a bag with our pyjamas in, so as soon as swimming was over, we could shower and change into them, ready for bed. Then, we'd get chips with tons of salt and vinegar on the way home. That was my kind of evening, and I looked forward to it every week.

The pyjama packing is a tradition I've kept up with my own kids. I've always got them in my bag, so if we're out late at someone's house, I can get the younger ones changed and ready for bed when they get in. I always get the kids' school uniforms laid out and prepared in the morning, so there's no mad dash – socks, boxers, shoes, bags – it's all laid out neatly and ready for them, which makes the mornings flow. I guess I've inherited these two traits from my parents – routine and forward planning.

We did a lot as a family, and although we didn't go on loads of big fancy holidays, we did go on some wonderful and eventful trips together. When my dad took his pension early because of a back injury, he wanted to take us all to Florida and Disneyland.

While we were there, there were no limits, and Dad spoiled us rotten.

Mum was a bit more practical and felt she had to rein him in a bit. 'They can't have everything, Tony!'

'But it's the magic kingdom; just let them enjoy it,' Dad reasoned, while we filled our shopping baskets in the gift shops.

He was made up with the idea of giving us kids that experience and determined to make it the best trip ever. As far as he was concerned, he'd worked hard for that money and wanted us all to enjoy it.

Before that, we'd only ever been to Spain a couple of times, and then there was the family caravan, which Dad bought for two hundred pounds when I was six. We'd visited my mum's cousin's caravan one weekend, and Dad spotted one for sale on the same site, so bought it on impulse.

Situated in the seaside town of West Kirby, it was pretty basic, but some of my best childhood memories are of the time we spent there.

Dad was still working then, and as soon as he'd finished on a Friday, Mum would put us in our pyjamas and we'd drive down there – it was about forty minutes away. We'd stay the whole weekend, sometimes driving back in time for Dad to go to Sunday evening mass while Mum got us kids ready for bed, all set for school on the Monday morning.

On one occasion, we were on our way back from the caravan when we broke down in the tunnel. Us kids were in our PJs as usual, but as well as that, Mum had just thrown a coat over her nightie to travel home in. She went ballistic thinking she was going to be stranded like that, rescued by the AA man in her nightwear.

The caravan itself had zero mod cons. There was no proper toilet, only a portable one that adults called the piss-pot. This thing doubled up as a handy step for me to climb on to get up to the top bunk, much to the annoyance of my mum.

'Get off that piss-pot before it goes over,' she'd scream at us.

She had the tiniest square footage of kitchen space, just enough for one person to fit in, but somehow, she managed to rustle up roast dinners, full-cooked breakfasts and big family meals without any complaints. We even managed to fit a whole other family inside. My auntie Ann, uncle John and cousins, Laura and Michael, spent many happy times there with us, and I have great memories of holidays with them.

As time passed, a few more of my aunties and uncles got caravans on the same site, and many good times were had. There was a beach nearby, well, I say a beach, it was some rocks and a bit of water with a few shells scattered about here and there. The site also boasted what we might now call an entertainment centre, which was basically a small hut where you brought your own ale, and there might be a singer or a game of bingo on. Still, it was absolute heaven for my brothers and me. We'd run around in the dunes, go crabbing or cockle picking, or race around the site on our bikes. I even found somewhere to go horse riding down there, and occasionally I'd help out, mucking out the stables.

We had the caravan for about six years, but despite my parents painting it and Mum making curtains for it, it was pretty run down in the end – it even had a few holes here and there. Eventually, it got chucked off the site as it wasn't in any fit state to be there, but my dad did get fifty pounds scrap for it.

Dad's parents, Dolly and Tommy, had a pub in Garston near the street where we lived when I was born. It was a proper old-school pub called The King's Vaults – what they used to call a working man's pub, I suppose. There was a core group of regulars who all knew one another and came in for their pints and for the lovely soft, floury balm cakes my nan put out on the bar every lunchtime.

Nan was the classic pub landlady. If there was a darts match on, she'd do all the food herself, and every morning when one of the cleaning ladies came in, Julie or Eileen, Nan would be downstairs cleaning along with her – bottoming the place every day, ready for opening. And like all the best pubs, they had many lock-ins and stay-behinds when their friends and regulars weren't quite ready to leave.

I was very close to my nan and grandad on my dad's side. I wouldn't like to say I was my nan's favourite, but we had a close and quite special relationship. I'd often stay with them during the six-week summer holidays, helping out around the pub – well, I thought I was helping out anyway. As a younger teenager, I'd be cleaning glasses behind the bar and collecting tips from the regulars, who'd give me a pound here and there. I'd save it all up in a tip jar throughout the summer and then go and spend it all on something special before the holidays ended.

That's one of the things I remember most about growing up in that environment, the generosity of Liverpool people. Most people who came into the pub didn't have an awful lot, but when Nan and Grandad hosted a charity night or held a collection for something, they always found something to give.

I have so many memories of their pub. One of my fondest is the time I made a programme for Channel 5 – in 2005, when I was nineteen. The show was a bit of a mixed bag; it followed me trying to find a dress for the National TV Awards but had a sprinkling of my day-to-day life thrown in for good measure. Some of my mates were in it, and I thought it was great at the time – although I'm not sure we could stand to watch it now. Back then, though, it was a big thing for us, so we arranged a premiere screening at The King's Vaults. All my friends and family turned out, and Wayne's cousin James, who was a singer, came down and did a turn. We had a brilliant night, and my friends who'd never been to the pub loved it.

'Oh, we'll have to come here more often; it's like being in The Rovers,' one of them said as she left.

I have so many memories of that pub, which struggled when the smoking ban came about in 2007. It closed in 2009, when Grandad wasn't quite as fit as he once was, but even then they still lived above it, and I'd still visit them there.

All my dad's family lived close to the pub, and I spent a lot of time at his younger sister Tracy's house. I always viewed her as my cool, trendy auntie. I often stayed with her, and she'd take me shopping for clothes. She always wore great clothes and nice shoes. I was always in my element when I was with her – fashion heaven! There was always a strong bond between us; Tracy was someone I could confide in.

I have to admit I was difficult when it came to clothes; my mum will testify to that. As a young child, I never wanted toys or dolls on birthdays or for Christmas. I wanted clothes and shoes. A fabulous wardrobe! And if I didn't get what I wanted, I made my feelings known. Being as fabulously fashion-conscious as she was, Tracy, I felt, understood my love of fashion.

Compared to my Grandad Tommy, Grandad Bob, my mum's dad, was a different kettle of fish. With Mum being the youngest of eight kids, he was quite an old grandad; in fact, my mum has a few nieces and nephews who are pretty close to her in age. We knew Grandad Bob loved us; he just didn't express it. He might tell us 'well done' if he felt it was deserved, but I don't remember him ever telling us that he loved us, like Grandad Tommy would. Bob wasn't really one for showing his feelings.

From when I was about four, Mum and Dad took over mum's old family home in Croxteth, which still belonged to Bob. He was moving in with his girlfriend, Kathy, in a high-rise flat not too far away.

Our house in Croxteth was always a busy one. With Mum's many siblings plus all their kids, the extended family descended on us every Saturday. Joe was the naughty one of the three of us kids, always kicking off and causing a fuss about something. My memories of him on those Saturdays involve him getting shouted at and told off for various antics or stirring up trouble between the kids. In the afternoons, Grandad Bob and the men would go off to the pub down the street while Mum would rustle up something delicious in the kitchen to feed everyone – a pan of pea soup, some scones or a curry. When she couldn't be bothered to cook, my cousins and I would run to the local chippy and come back with armfuls of chips while Mum stood buttering slices of bread or barm cakes for the chips to go inside – you can't beat a chip barm.

Although Bob had technically moved out, he ended up coming back to live with us several times over the years. This would generally be after he'd rowed with Kathy, and she'd chucked him out. When this happened, my dad would have to drive over to Kathy's flat to pick up him and a load of bin bags and then bring him back to ours. Luckily, it was a four-bedroom house, so we had the space, and we always kept Grandad Bob's room vacant because we never knew when he might turn up with his bin bags and exercise bike – which also went back and forth a fair few times.

Eventually, Bob lived with us full time right up until he passed away. It started with just a fall in the bathroom when I was around eleven. We didn't think it was anything too serious, but he was taken to the hospital in an ambulance. We weren't sure how long he was going to be there.

A few days later, one of my cousins, Danielle, came to meet me from school, which was completely out of the ordinary.

'What's going on? Why have you come to meet me?' I asked on the way home.

'Oh, no special reason,' she said, but her face was drained of colour so I knew something was up.

When I got home, my auntie Kathleen, Mum's sister, was at the house – a feeling of dread came over me.

'What's going on?' I asked again.

'Your grandad has died, love,' Kathleen said.

He'd suffered a heart attack in hospital. It had been unexpected and quite sudden.

Everyone was shocked, but this was my first experience

of someone I knew dying, and it was horrible. During the days leading up to the funeral, when Grandad Bob was laid out in wake at home, our house was suddenly packed again for the rosary service – a Catholic tradition – held the night before the funeral. It was just like those lovely, busy Saturdays when I was little and all Mum's brothers and sisters came for a visit. I do have some funny, fond memories of my Grandad Bob. I used to twitch my nose as a kid, and he would always say to me, 'Don't do that, Coleen, you'll get stuck like that and end up looking like Miss Piggy.'

It used to make me laugh, but I have now got a lop-sided nostril because of that twitch, so he knew what he was talking about!

Also, his bedroom was the only one with a full-length mirror, so I'd constantly be bursting in without any warning, just so I could try outfits on and see how they looked before I went out.

Poor Bob would often be napping or sitting quietly reading. 'What are you doing now, Coleen?' he'd say.

'I'm just lookin',' was always the reply – every single time. 'I'm just lookin'.'

When he died, I wrote a message on a card to him. I miss you Grandad, and I was always just looking.

Chapter Two

As young kids, we all went to our parish school, Saint Teresa's, and to church every Sunday. Mum and Dad both come from Catholic families, and although Mum's family wasn't big into the church, she attended a Catholic school. Dad's family weren't massive churchgoers either, but he took it upon himself to go from a young age. In fact, he was an altar boy, despite the rough-and-ready area he came from and despite some of his mates taking the mick. Whenever they were out on the street, and Dad told them he had to go to mass, they'd all cross themselves. Dad didn't care what his mates thought; he loved being an altar boy and going to mass – he owned it. That's something I've learned from my dad and have tried to pass on to the boys.

'Don't be worrying what anyone else thinks,' I'll tell them. 'Concentrate on yourself.'

Of course, that sometimes backfires. When I saw Kai's exam results a few months back, I asked him, 'What did everyone else get?'

'Why are you asking what everyone else got,' he said,

quick as a flash. 'You're always telling me not to bother about everyone else.'

Fair play to him.

Dad still has a strong faith and still goes to church most days. When we were little, we loved going to the 11.15 a.m. children's mass on a Sunday morning, where we'd sing and read with all the other kids and familiar faces from school. If ever we missed that, we'd go to the six o'clock mass, which was quieter and a lot more serious.

I remember Joe, Anthony and I getting the giggles sometimes during six o'clock mass, and while I always loved a good giggle, this was not the place and time for it. We'd always get that certain glare of my dad, which said, *Stop it right now! Just wait till you get out of here!*

As we got older, we weren't always keen on going so much. In fact, I went through a stage of feeling a bit embarrassed by it. I'd be staying at my mate's houses for Saturday-night sleepovers, and Dad would remind me that he was picking me up for church in the morning. If it was just my close mates at the sleepover, I was honest about where I was going, but if there was anyone new in the mix, I'd tell them I was going to dancing or swimming. Terrible really!

Still, first communion was always a significant event in our house and, true to form, there was always a big party afterwards, with friends and family piling into the house until the early hours, singing and having a good time in the back garden.

Once we were sixteen, we were given the option of whether we wanted to go or not. I still went fairly regularly, and we're still a churchgoing family. The only thing is, the boys play football on Saturdays and Sundays, and as they're part of teams and academies, attendance is very important, so it's not always possible. They have all been christened, though, and the oldest two have made their communion. Wayne's also from a Catholic family, so it's something that's been a part of our family from both sides.

The school Kai got into is diverse, and their attitude to religion is progressive. They have assemblies for each religion, but any child can go regardless of their faith. So aside from the Christian assembly, Kai might go to a Jewish one with one friend or a Hindu one with another. It's a wonderful way to do it, and I believe it helps the kids through life, understanding other ways and cultures.

As my brothers and I got a bit older, Mum got involved in a charity that took sick and underprivileged children away on trips – they might go to Lourdes in France, Euro Disney, and sometimes even Orlando. The idea was to give them a trip of a lifetime, something they would never have been able to experience otherwise. Eventually, Dad got involved with the trips as well. He'd suffered with prolapsed discs and, being a bricklayer, it was better for him to take redundancy and retire early. Over time, their voluntary work with the children became increasingly important to them. It was something they both loved, which became a big part of our family life. Mum's sister, my auntie Shelagh, was always on hand to look after me and my brothers, moving in with us when Mum and Dad went away on trips. I'd been close to her ever since I was a baby, so I was always happy when she came to stay.

Eventually, Mum wanted to take things further and try respite care and fostering. This would mean taking care of some sick or disabled children at weekends now and again or during school holidays to give their parents a break. It wasn't something my parents undertook lightly. I was twelve when they sat Joe, Anthony and me down in the living room, asking us how we felt about the idea of other children coming to stay with us at home from time to time. Coming from a big family, I suppose we were used to being around lots of other kids, so the idea didn't faze us. We listened, we nodded, we just accepted it. My dad said recently that he still can't believe how well we all adjusted to it as a family; a lot of kids would probably have found it difficult to see their parents dividing their attention in that way – especially when there were already three of us. He was right, I suppose, but at the same time, it made me think about how amazing and giving my parents were – having three young kids of their own to look after yet still holding out their hands to other families who needed help.

The children who came to stay with us had varying disabilities; some needed more hands-on care, and some were less mobile than others. Eventually, Mum and Dad started fostering children for more extended periods. Kids who were waiting to find a more permanent family situation, and again, my brothers and I just went with the flow and accepted it. We knew our parents enjoyed doing it, and I never felt like they were too busy for me or that I was going without. They seemed to have enough time and love for all of us, and that was what mattered.

When I was about fifteen, in 2001, Mum was asked about a little girl called Rosie, who'd been removed from her home along with her brother and sister. She was being separated from her siblings because she needed such specific care, so taking her in would be a more long-term commitment. Mum and Dad decided it was something they'd like to do and agreed that Rosie, who was only two, could come and live with us for as long as she needed to.

Having two brothers, I was dead excited about having a baby sister. I suppose I'm very much like Mum in that way – a girly girl! I loved babysitting and being about little ones, so as far as I was concerned, Rosie's arrival was something to look forward to.

Rosie could crawl and eat but couldn't walk or speak, although she would make noises and sounds – one of which was like 'Mama'. We all thought, as did the foster home, she'd been badly neglected and hadn't yet developed all her skills. The feeling was that she would get better with time and the proper care. Despite her difficulties, she fitted in right away and quickly became part of the family; she'd look up at us with her big, beautiful green eyes, and we all quickly fell in love with her.

After a while, Mum realised there was more to Rosie's condition than neglect and started looking into it. She read up on various illnesses and disorders that mirrored Rosie's behaviour and her condition. Eventually, she came across Rett's syndrome, which affects brain development, causing mental and physical disability. It's a very rare genetic disorder, almost always found in girls, and it's not something that can be cured; in fact, it gets worse as time goes on, with children losing what little ability they do have.

'I'm sure this is what Rosie has,' she told my dad, and as it turned out, she was right.

I think because it's so rare, Rosie's condition had gone undiagnosed, but with Mum's determination and diligence, that diagnosis finally came.

It was a blow because Rett's is a lifetime condition and highly debilitating, but by then, we'd all become so attached to Rosie. There was a bond there with all of us, and I could tell that Mum and Dad didn't want the day to come when they'd have to say goodbye to her. Ultimately, they decided to adopt her legally, a long and challenging legal procedure that took years. But in the end, that's what happened. Rosie really was part of our family, my adopted baby sister.

It was hard work for Mum and Dad, but now she was theirs, she was ours, and we all loved her. As she got older,

Rosie's lack of mobility meant changes to the house – making a bedroom and installing a bathroom for her downstairs, making sure there was wheelchair access where it was needed. As she grew and got heavier, getting her in and out of bed and baths became more challenging, so we had equipment and hoists to help with those tasks. Holidays had to be meticulously thought through and planned, with things like her wheelchair, oxygen and feeding tubes considered. There were also times when she'd get sick, and my parents didn't sleep for nights on end taking care of her.

Despite everything, it all just seemed to flow. She'd become part of us, and Mum and Dad would do whatever it took to make sure she was comfortable and felt loved, and without a word of complaint. Nothing really changed in many ways; we still did everything we always had as a family. My brothers and I never felt like Rosie took our mum and dad away from us because they still did everything and more for us, and never loved us one bit less than they would have if Rosie hadn't been there. Even more admirable – and pretty unbelievable – is that when Rosie was first with us, they still took in and cared for other disadvantaged and disabled children, who came and stayed with us for short periods.

I suppose that's a testament to the people they are; if I've inherited even a quarter of their qualities, I consider myself very fortunate.

I loved it when there was a baby in the house, and there were times, for whatever reason, when Mum had to bring newborns home straight from the hospital. This was always a significant event because ours was the first home they'd come to, their very first environment, their first taste of life, of love and of care. I'd be in my element, of course, acting like a mother hen and getting involved. Over time, we had three babies at the house: two girls and a boy. Bryan, the boy, is sixteen now, and we still see him. He still visits Mum and Dad at their house. Bryan's adoptive parents wanted us to be in his life as he didn't have any blood siblings, and Mum and Dad were more than happy with that. There's also a young lad, Jake, who has Down's syndrome. He stayed with us when he was little, and we still see him; in fact, my brother Joe takes him out all the time. They'll go to bowling or to Joe's local league football matches and Jake will sometimes stay over with Joe and his family. Everyone loves him.

I like the idea that, as a family, we've been a part of so many kids' lives and helped them in difficult stages of their journey. The whole family got involved, too.

Some of my aunties and uncles attended organised trips with Mum, and my auntie Shelagh ended up doing respite fostering as well. In fact, Rosie would sometimes go to her for the odd weekend. At other times, my cousin Lisa would help out with Rosie's overnight care. The extended family saw Rosie as their niece or cousin, and no different to Anthony, Joe and me. I'm not sure I can think of many families where that would be the case.

Looking back, it was such a massive part of our lives, but it all felt quite natural to us at the time. I have such admiration for my parents for doing all that while bringing up children of their own. They've always known they were doing a good thing, but more than that, they did it because they loved doing it.

As Rosie grew up, her condition progressed. She had epilepsy, meaning she might fit several times a day, and sometimes her breathing got so bad she needed oxygen. There were times when Mum and Dad were fraught with worry, nursing her through some horrible infection or illness, but there were other times when she'd go for a good long spell without anything going seriously wrong. Even then, she needed twenty-four-hour care.

Still, every day, Rosie got picked up by bus and taken to school – she had a one-on-one carer dedicated just to her. She had this cheeky way about her, and despite everything, we were convinced she knew exactly what we were talking about.

She could be crafty too and didn't like going to school very much. The school phoned Mum one day and told her Rosie wasn't well.

'We're going to take her to the hospital. Will you meet us there?'

Of course, Mum and Dad went flying to action stations, and by the time the ambulance reached the hospital, they were there waiting for it. As Rosie was lowered out of the ambulance in her wheelchair, she spotted Mum and Dad and burst out laughing. It turned out she wasn't ill; she was trying to skive school, pretending to be sick. As well as that, if someone fell over or banged an arm or leg on something in the house, she'd laugh loudly. Consequently, my dad, always one for going over the top, would throw himself on the floor just because he loved seeing her laugh. So much of her knew what was going on; she just couldn't always communicate with the world.

Down the line, she started going to Claire House Children's Hospice for respite care. This was so Mum and Dad could have a break, get some uninterrupted sleep, and even take Joe, Anthony and me away for weekends.

Claire House was such an amazing place which, as a family, we've continued to support in thanks for all they did for Rosie and us.

In 2006, I participated in a TV documentary focusing on the funding crisis and cuts facing so many hospices. On ITV's *Tonight With Trevor McDonald*, I talked about Rosie's struggles and how the kind of help we were getting from Claire House was so desperately needed. Similar charities around the country help so many families and children, but they're simply underfunded, some have even been cut altogether. Following the broadcast of the show, the prime minister pledged an extra 27 million pounds over three years for children's hospices, and agreed to launch an independent review into their future funding.

Chapter Three

My passions as a teenager were drama and dancing. Outside school, I went to a dance class and a drama school and, as part of The Harlequin Roadshow, I danced in shows all around the country, including performances at Sadler's Wells and Her Majesty's Theatre in London.

It was having an audience I really got a kick out of, seeing people enjoying something I was doing. I also liked the idea that I could be someone else for a while, showing different sides of me.

Through these after-school activities, I was introduced to a whole new group of friends, which meant my social circle was now bursting at the seams – and pretty varied too. I was confident and got on well with people, both in and out of school. It wasn't something I set out to achieve; it just happened naturally. Looking back, I think it was because my mum and dad always strove to instil a sense of fairness in me. They taught us kids that everyone is equal and should be treated as such. Having several different groups of mates rather than sticking to one clique helped me understand that. I had my study mates, who were in the top sets at school with me, but then I also had other groups I hung around with outside of school, who had other interests I shared. To me, one group wasn't better than or superior to the other, and I flitted quite happily from one to the other.

As I got more into the idea of performing, my auntie Shelagh's sister-in-law Bernadette Foley was in *Brookside*, playing a character called Margi Shadwick. For those who don't know, that was a TV soap opera on Channel 4, huge throughout the eighties and nineties.

Bernadette recognised my love of performing and told me, 'You need to get an agent, Coleen.'

I managed to find one to take me on, and although not much came of it, she did get me a couple of walk-on parts in *Hollyoaks*. In one episode I played a girl at school who gets paint poured into her bag by one of the main characters. I don't think I actually had a name, but as far as I'm concerned, it was a bit more than a walk-on, as there was acting involved. Well, a bit of acting. If anything, the experience only heightened my love of performing. I loved being on the set, watching everyone rush around with their various jobs and seeing how everything worked. Plus, I didn't have to travel far because it was filmed right there in Liverpool.

My other passion was clothes and fashion, which didn't diminish as I blossomed into my early teens. As soon as

I was old enough, I was keen to earn my own money so I could keep my wardrobe up to scratch. Firstly, I babysat for Mum's friends who lived over the road from our house. It was a once-a-week thing; they'd go out to the pub on a Friday night, and I'd run over, sit with the kids and earn a fiver. Mum was happy for me to go, as she could practically see me from the window and knew what I was getting up to. Sort of.

Not content with babysitting, I'd go through the house while I was there every week, cleaning it from top to bottom while the kids were in bed. Can you imagine a child who loves cleaning and does it voluntarily? I'm not sure why but I was mad for it. I was pretty forthright, too; if I felt things were in the wrong place or didn't look right, I'd re-arrange them to my satisfaction, no messing. I'm sure, more than once, my mum's friend must have thought, *Cheeky bitch, re-organising my home*, but she never said anything. Probably because she was getting such a good deal from me – babysitter and cleaner for a fiver, while they were out drinking.

My aunties did contract cleaning, and one of their jobs was the chalets at Pontins in Southport. At fourteen, I wasn't technically old enough to do the job, but armed with a fake National Insurance number, I'd get onto the minibus with all the other cleaners and head off. We worked in pairs – I'd team up with my auntie Pat – and we'd go around tidying and scrubbing our allotted chalets, some of which were disgusting. I didn't mind. Aside from getting paid, I was getting my regular and necessary fix of doing somebody else's housework. I know, I'm weird.

When I wasn't doing drama or dance, I was doing what so many kids did in Liverpool back in those days, hanging out on the street. Back then, I hung around with my cousin Clair. We'd been close since I was young, and I spent a lot of time at my auntie Pat and uncle Peter's house – Clair's mum and dad. They had three girls, so it was a completely different atmosphere to our house. I loved being around Clair and her sisters, Kelly and Danielle, who were older than us. We'd watch them getting ready to go out, and on occasion they'd even take Clair and I out with them, which always made us feel dead grown-up.

Clair and I were friends with Amy-Louise, who lived over the road from me. The three of us were as thick as thieves, all hanging around in Norris Green, about a fifteen- to twenty-minute walk from where we lived in Croxteth. If we weren't milling around outside a parade of shops called The Strand, there was always the park or the local McDonald's. We always seemed to have such a great time, just chatting and doing nothing very much, but whenever I had something to study or practise for, or if I had an upcoming exam, I'd make sure I stayed in do it.

'Oh, why aren't you coming out, Coleen?' the girls would complain. 'Just come out for a bit.'

I was always dedicated to what I was doing, though.

I wanted everything to be the best it could possibly be. So I'd usually stick to my guns and stay home.

That's not to say there wasn't the odd bit of misbehaving, I wasn't a perfect angel by any means. When I was about thirteen, I went with Clair and my friend Kate to an under-sixteens' disco called The Swarm, held in The Conti nightclub on a Friday night. Of course, being an underage event meant there was no alcohol, so we took it upon ourselves to do a bit of pre-match drinking on the way there. Not the best idea for a bunch of thirteen-year-old girls, but it was one of those things kids tended to do back then if they could get away with it, as we thought we could. We persuaded some woman to go into the shop and buy us cider – well, I say persuaded, we actually bribed her with a pound and the promise of some poppadoms from the Indian restaurant next door. Then we drank the cider on the number 14 bus on the way to the club. It wasn't the first time I'd drunk alcohol on the down low, but it was the most memorable, and for all the wrong reasons.

We had the best time at the disco, with plenty of over-enthusiastic dancing, meeting up with friends and a healthy amount of gossip and laughter. It felt exciting all being out together, dancing at a proper nightclub – almost like a taste of things to come. I remember how giggly and happy we were, piling into Kate's dad's car afterwards, still buzzing from the cider, talking nineteen to the dozen. Then, as Kate's dad took off into the night, we all started singing to the radio – 'Dancing Queen' by Abba. Honestly, I felt fine and, I have to say, quite normal, although I might not have looked it.

Watching the lights of Liverpool whizz past the car window, it dawned on me that I still had forty-five minutes left before I was expected home – result! Not wanting my night to end, I asked Kate's dad to drop Clair and me off, where I knew a group of my mates were hanging out. Why go home when there was still more fun to be had? So, Clair and I jumped out of the car and hung out a while longer with our mates, while Kate's dad took her home.

When I eventually arrived home, weaving my way along our street, my mum, dad and brothers were standing in the front garden waiting for me. If I told you my mum and dad didn't look the happiest I'd ever seen them look, that would be an understatement. Still, I put on a brave face and headed in anyway.

'What's going on here?' I said with a smile.

'Get inside,' my dad said.

'Why, what's up?'

Once I was in, all hell broke loose.

'Right, what have you been doing?' Dad yelled at me.

'Nothing, I've been at the disco; we've had a great night.'

'Well, you stink of drink, so where did that come from,' he said.

'What do you mean, I stink of drink?'

I must have made a right mess of trying to lie my way out of it because then he said, 'And you're not making any sense.'

At the time, I thought I was as sober as a judge, but I was clearly all over the place. The more I tried to explain myself, the worse it sounded to my dad.

'I'm disgusted with you, Coleen, drinking on the streets, absolutely disgusted.'

Meanwhile, my brothers, who were only young, thought this was the best thing ever. Finally, their annoying, bossy sister was getting her comeuppance, and they were loving every second of it.

I've got friends now who might let their older teenagers have a small glass of something under their supervision, but back then, in our social circle, it wasn't the norm for people as young as I was to try alcohol. My parents were fuming because I'd gone behind their backs and done something I knew they'd disapprove of.

For a while, I had no idea how my mum and dad even knew we'd been secretly drinking. It turned out Kate had been sick in the car, so her dad had cottoned on. Worried because he'd dropped me off on the street intoxicated, they phoned my parents to let them know the score, and make sure I'd got home safely. Of course, Kate's parents had done the right thing, ensuring everyone involved was OK, but at the time, getting caught like that felt like a friggin' nightmare.

The upshot was that I was grounded as well as getting a proper telling-off. The following Monday I saw Kate at school, and we rolled our eyes at one another, acknowledging our shared horror and shame at being caught.

That's not to say I was completely reformed after that. Some of my friends and I went through a phase of camping out overnight. The thing is, I never let on to my parents that I was outdoors all night under canvas; instead, I told them I was staying at a friend's place.

We had some nerve back then. One of our friends lived on a close built around a green; sometimes, we'd set up our tents there. Once we were all set up, we'd go into her house, phone our parents and tell them we were in for the evening, safe and sound, before heading back out to the green where we spent the rest of the night. The funny part was that the friend whose house it was wasn't even allowed to go with us. She'd have to go up to bed, face like thunder, while we were all camping on the grass in front of her house having a whale of a time.

It started off with just us girls, but eventually, the boys pitched their own tent on the green. We'd sit around, talking, giggling and playing music – someone always had a radio or cassette player. Then, in the early hours, we'd wander down The Lancs, which is what we called the East Lancs Road, to the petrol station, where we'd buy drinks and snacks to take back to camp. A few of the boys used to rob the milk and orange juice off people's doorsteps.

Sometimes, we camped out in a field over the back of the sports centre, and there was one occasion when the police turned up to move us on. Generally, though, there was no real trouble. Although I'm not entirely sure Mum and Dad knew anything about my secret overnight camp-outs – I guess they will now.

That was pretty tame anyway. Some girls in my year were sneaking out to nightclubs and getting away with it. I was never that naughty. Some of those girls had older sisters, but in my family, I *was* the older sister. Whatever wayward behaviour occurred, I was always going to be the first one to try it and bloody well get caught for it, and being the first, it was always going to seem like a serious matter. By the time my brothers got up to mischief, my parents had become more accustomed to it.

As time went on, I started going to a youth club attached to Croxteth high school, which some of my mates attended. This was another new group I immersed myself in, and for a while, I went back and forth between them and the crowd in Norris Green. Eventually, I veered towards the Croxteth group, and some of the other Norris Green crowd went their own way too. There was no bad blood, it was just something that happened naturally. The youth club wasn't anything fancy – there was a room with a CD player, and you could get a cheese toastie for about 50p, which was a good deal in my book. The team who ran the place were good people. It's not like we were in street gangs or doing anything criminal, but they did provide us with somewhere to go rather than just hanging around on street corners and getting into trouble, as kids sometimes do. It was nice to have somewhere we could all go and be together, just doing standard teenage stuff, or even just getting out of the rain.

I remember bringing in the video of one of my school productions – we all sat around and watched it, and I was dead proud of myself. Other times, the girls would practise dance routines while the boys played in the games rooms. They were good times and, I suppose, the start of my social life and making friends, some of whom I'm still very close to now.

My mates from the Croxteth posse always had nicknames. They got saddled with them when we were kids, and they're still bandied around to this day. Catherine Miller is Cilla – it rhymes with Miller, but she also loved playing *Blind Date* at school, taking on the role of Liverpool legend, Cilla Black.

Her parents, Rose and John, weren't all that keen when one of us would turn up at their house and ask, 'Is Cilla in?'

They'd give me a look and then shout up the stairs, 'CATHERINE!'

Natalie Fenlan is Fen – always the life and soul of the party and naturally funny. Laura Knibb is Knibby, and Louise Brenan is Brenda.

She's definitely not keen on the name that's stuck with her all these years and goes mad when people she's known for years think it's her actual name. Quite often, when we've gone out and met new people, she'll issue a stern warning: 'Don't call me Brenda in front of anyone; call me by my proper name!'

One of my friends, Laura, was always Chopper – she was friends with Wayne before I knew her, and he'd given her the nickname. I don't really have a nickname that's stuck with the girls, although some of them call me Colly Mc. My dad used to call me Pippy, after the children's fiction character, Pippi Longstocking, because I was strong and stood for no messing, and my nan, uncle Peter and Catherine's brother John all call me Colly Wobbles. I'm not sure where that one came from.

The girls and I all still see one another now, and although so many years have passed, it doesn't seem long since we were all walking the streets together or eating cheese toasties in the youth club. They still make me laugh, and sometimes we act as daft and mad as we did as kids when we all get together. The best thing about them is that they're always there for me, and we're a very protective bunch. If somebody picks on one of us, they'll usually have to deal with all of us. I find that's a common trait in people from Liverpool, that loyalty. They're a wonderful group of friends, and I consider myself very lucky to have them.

*

Overall, I had a pretty good social life during my teenage years. Yes, I might have hung around on the street and done a bit of underage drinking, but I also had my dance classes, made sure all my schoolwork was up to scratch, and still spent lots of quality time with my family. I was streetwise without being in the mix of everything going on, so I never got into any serious trouble. As far as the life of a teenager went, there was a good balance.

When I think about my eldest son, Kai, who's fourteen, I sometimes wonder if he's missing out on some of the things Wayne and I did as kids, things that came naturally to us. It's nobody's fault, but my children's social lives are pretty organised. Kai doesn't hang out on the street because there are no streets to hang out on where we live – we're in the middle of the countryside behind gates. If he's going to friends', I'll drive him there because it's what we've always done, and there's no other way to get around. At his school, plenty of kids live in regular streets or estates who can knock on for one another and play out, but that's not the case for him. He's not out on his bike with his mates every night or hanging out in the park all weekend, as I was. That said, he's extremely fortunate in many other ways and gets to do things many other kids his age don't get to do and, of course, as he gets older, things will change.

I've tried to expose our boys to as much normality as possible because my upbringing and family life are the things that have kept me grounded. Whenever we visit family back in Liverpool, the boys get stuck in with all their cousins and their cousin's friends, and they love getting in the mix of everything. I think that same grounding also helped Wayne and me as a couple – especially a couple in the public eye. We grew up as regular kids with loving families and good mates, and we've carried all that with us, despite the enormous changes in our lives over the years. This approach means we've enjoyed the best of both worlds and can comfortably mix with people from all walks of life.

The boys get that through family and school, and the older ones through their football academy. They're mixing with all these amazing kids from different areas and backgrounds. That's important to us.

When I go back to the area where I grew up, I feel like nothing's really changed. Most people I know don't treat me any differently, and I like to think I'm the same toward them. I have the same group of best friends as I did back then, and I've held on to the same values my parents instilled in me. Of course, you'll always get the odd person saying, 'Oh, she's changed,' but in truth, those people have changed towards me. They assume that because of everything that comes with my life, I can't possibly be the same person or even a normal person. It's an unfair assumption, but one it's hard to fight against. You just have to accept it.

Chapter Four

Wayne's cousin, another Claire, was a year below me at school. I've known of her since I was little. My dad ran the local boxing gym with her dad, and our families both went to the same church, so we all knew one another.

That said, Claire and I weren't really friends when we were younger; it was her brother Thomas I hung around with, in Norris Green, where their family lived. Once I'd gravitated to the group that hung out around Croxteth, I got to know Claire a bit more, and eventually, we became good mates.

Wayne, meanwhile, was part of another group that hung around very close to our house. He went to an all-boys school around the corner from my school, which was all girls, and there was many an afternoon when Wayne and a few of his mates would either finish early or bunk off their last lesson to mill around my school gates, ready for our exit.

In summer, we wore pale lemon open-necked shirts, and the boys would sometimes stand on top of the nearby garages and throw water balloons or squirt water pistols at us, so our shirts would become wet and see-through. You could always guarantee some poor flustered teacher from our place dashing across the playground and out of the school gates, screaming for the boys to go away.

I'd see Wayne most nights on my way home, and sometimes I'd stop for a chat with him and his pals. As they were always near our house, I could sometimes get away with staying out an extra fifteen minutes because I was practically in shouting distance of my mum and dad, so of course I took advantage.

Wayne was always a bit of a cheeky one. From as far back as I can remember, he was asking me the same questions.

'Would you go out with me, Coleen?' or 'Can I have a date?'

And I'd always laugh it off. OK, so I'd kissed a couple of boys by then – all very innocent – but I'd never done the boyfriend/girlfriend thing. I just didn't have the headspace for it, what with my studies and after-school activities. My diary was full.

My friends were horrified at the idea that I had better things to do than go on dates.

'I haven't got time,' I'd say, 'I'm too busy.'

'Busy doing what?'

'My dancing, my studies. I'll get a boyfriend when I'm good and ready, OK?'

I don't remember wanting to be somebody's girlfriend at the time; other things were more important – like my exams.

'Maybe I'll go on dates with someone once I've done my GCSEs,' I'd tell my friends.

I was thinking ahead, but at the same time, very non-committal.

The more I got to know Wayne, the more I liked him, but something in me told me he was a handful – talk about female intuition. I could tell he was a bit naughty; he liked the girls and always looked older than he was – he had a beard at fifteen. The most appealing thing about him was his confidence and also his determination. I could tell he liked me, and the way he carried on, I knew he wasn't likely to give up until I agreed to a date.

The summer after I'd finished my GCSEs, we did start seeing one another a bit more regularly. He was hard to avoid, to be honest, as I usually had to walk past him on my way home every evening.

One afternoon, while I was strolling happily along the street, I bumped into him by the chip shop. He'd just got his first pair of contact lenses, which he was struggling with.

'I can't get these in,' he said. 'Do you know how to put them in?'

'You can't do it out in the fresh air; they'll dry out.' I wore contact lenses from the age of twelve until I was twenty-one and had laser treatment, so felt able to advise.

'Well, come in here,' Wayne said, gesturing towards a phone box. 'You can help me.'

As far as making a move goes, it wasn't the classiest, but I suppose it was at least original. *Come in the phone box and help me get my contact lenses in!*

We never did get them in.

Another day, on my way home from Croxteth, I went into the chip shop where Wayne was hanging out.

'I'm gonna marry her,' he told the lady behind the counter, with such confidence, you'd almost believe it.

'No, you're not,' I said, blushing like beetroot.

He was always coming out with stuff like that, declarations of love and marriage, and I'd always go dead shy. Secretly, though, I liked his confidence and the fact that he knew what he wanted.

Still, I always stood firm. 'That's not happening.'

Coming back from a bike ride with Claire one evening, my bike chain came off, and I couldn't get it back on. As we were pushing our bikes along the street, Wayne appeared as he always seemed to.

'Can you fix the chain on her bike?' Claire asked.

I nudged her in the ribs, embarrassed.

'I can fix it, yeah.' I think he was made up to be asked.

'Go on, then,' I said.

Wayne has never been what you'd call a handyman, but he's always been good at all the typical boys' stuff, so could easily mend a bike chain. In return for his services, he asked me out on a date again. I still wasn't convinced, but we chatted for a while, and before I knew it, he was following me home to borrow my video of *Grease* which, looking back, was probably just a ploy, but I went for it anyway. After I'd handed over the video, we went for a stroll, ending up in the local churchyard. That's when we had our first kiss, around the back of the Queen of Martyrs. It had been a long time coming, but his persistence had finally paid off.

After that, I gave in and told Claire I would go on a proper date with Wayne. The look on her face told me this was a massive relief for her, as he'd been going on at her for months to persuade me. Once she'd gotten the green light, she couldn't wait to rush off, tell him the good news and lift the burden from her shoulders.

Before the date – a trip to the cinema to see *Austin Powers*, I told Mum what was going on.

'I think you'd better ask your dad first,' she said.

'Must I?'

I was sixteen by then, but, in the end, we agreed it was best to ask in case I got home later than usual.

'Who are you going with?' Dad wanted to know.

'Wayne.' This was the first time I'd ever even mentioned him as a potential boyfriend.

Dad eyed me suspiciously. 'You can go as long as you sit at the back and he sits at the front,' he said.

With Dad's blessing, or at least his version of one,

Wayne and I went off to the cinema followed by a dinner date at the local McDonald's. I could tell he was committed right from the off; he was very attentive and he'd even ditched the trackies and splashed out on a new outfit. Wayne had already had a couple of girlfriends, but this was a whole new world for me. A proper date and a potential relationship. It felt like a big step.

It's funny; I'd never been one to talk about boys to my dad. I suppose it's because I didn't want him to feel like somebody was taking me away from him. In his father-of-the-bride speech at our wedding, Dad likened his earliest meetings with Wayne to the movie *Meet the Fockers*. I'm not sure it was quite that full-on, but I do remember one night when Wayne and some mates came to ours to watch the football with Joe and Anthony – they'd all hung out together long before I started dating him. After the footy, Wayne switched the TV to the Channel 4 show *Eurotrash*, which was this brash, late-night magazine show – very rude and always full of sex stories and naked people. A few minutes after it came on, my dad walked into the living room and went completely off his head.

'Don't be having this on in my house; it's disgusting. Get it off!'

I don't remember what was on the screen at the time of his untimely entry, but it was probably someone with their bits out, as was usual for that particular show. Wayne was mortified, but that was my dad. Sometimes, he'd even go off if I was watching *Brookside*, thinking it was all sorts of terrible. Wow, when I think about what kids watch now, *Brookside* was positively innocent. He spotted a men's magazine in Joe's room once – it was only *Zoo* or *Nuts* or something, but Dad yelled at him, 'Don't be bringing porn into this house!'

He was pretty old school in that way, so yes, Wayne had his work cut out when it came to winning my dad over. Dad was strict compared to most of my friends' parents, but it was always balanced. As kids, we had boundaries, but we were also given choices and made to see why certain types of behaviour were not the best way forward.

Not long after Wayne and I started dating, I got a Saturday job in the high-street store New Look. This was the perfect gig for me. It was fashion, I was getting paid, plus we got a fifty per cent discount. Perfect! I was in the midst of my GCSEs then, so I could only work a few hours each week, but I loved it. My boss, Linsey, was a good one. She never made me sort the clear rail, where people hung up all the stuff they'd tried on but didn't buy – a chore all the staff there hated. Instead, she kept me on the shop floor or the till, doing the jobs I enjoyed. We've been friends ever since.

With Wayne's birthday coming up a few weeks after I'd started the New Look job, all my hard-earned wages went towards saving for his birthday present. I didn't make a lot; my dad probably spent more on petrol picking me up and dropping me off than I actually earned. Still, I managed to get him some headphones and an Armani jumper, which made me feel very grown up.

In those first few months of dating, Wayne and I did the same things all the other kids our age did. We hung around one another's houses or went to the chippy or maybe the cinema if we had the cash. I knew Wayne was mad into football, and from what I'd heard, he was good at it, not that I knew much about it. At the time, he was playing at Everton's youth academy, in the under-19s – he'd been with Everton since he was nine. Quite a few lads from the area went into the Liverpool or Everton youth teams, but not many of them shone through like Wayne ultimately did. Still, sixteen was incredibly young to play at that level; it's strange to think he was only two years older than my eldest is now. Consequently, there was a lot of attention on him and, eventually, on us as a couple.

On a damp, chilly morning in February 2002, Wayne arrived at our house to pick up the headphones I'd bought him, which he'd left there. He was dead excited, about to leave for his first England game against Australia at Upton Park in London. At sixteen, he was about to become the youngest senior international on the England squad, so he was big news.

There must have been photographers following him that morning, and after he'd picked up his headphones and left, they hung around to find out what mystery person lived in the house he'd just visited. Half an hour later, while I was on my way along the street to St John Bosco High Arts School, I was snapped, striding along looking terribly serious.

The photographer had done his best to be inconspicuous, hiding behind a raised car bonnet, but I'd spotted him anyway, directly across the road from where I was walking. After I got to school and told a couple of my mates, a buzz went around the place. Suddenly everyone seemed to know the gossip.

'Have yous heard? Coleen McLoughlin had some strange man taking pictures of her on her way to school this morning. Can you bloody believe it?'

It was the talk of the school that morning; so much so, that one of my teachers pulled me aside to have a word.

'Do you think we should call your mum and tell her what's happened?' she said.

It was such a strange situation; I don't think anyone knew what to do for the best. At the time, we didn't even know if the guy was a press photographer. In fact, for all I knew, he could have been some random taking pictures of schoolgirls.

My nan was the first one who spotted my picture in the papers the following weekend. Living in a pub, she bought all the papers, devouring them early before anyone else did. She loved them, and generally believed every word she read, even when I told her not to. She was like the local news, phoning us at seven in the morning some days. 'You'll never guess what I've just heard . . .'

On the morning in question, she phoned with an extra special news bulletin: 'Our Coleen's in the paper this morning!'

We lived next door to a newsagent, so I dashed out and grabbed a copy. Sure enough, there I was, striding along in my puffa coat, flapping in the breeze – my very first paparazzi shot. No real story went along with the picture, just a caption saying something like – 'This is the girl Wayne Rooney has been dating.' But that was the beginning of it all, and I must say, it all felt very strange.

Wayne made his first-team debut on 17 August 2002 in a 2–2 home draw against Spurs – aged sixteen. He was the second youngest player in the team's history to play a first-team match after Joe Royle in the 1960s. After the game, Wayne's entire family piled into the local pub, The Western, to celebrate. It was an exciting and memorable day for everyone. I recently found a scrapbook with the ticket to the first game I attended, which was not long after. I went along with his mum, and before kick-off, we met up with some of Wayne's other family members in the pub facing the ground.

It was quite a big thing for me, watching my first professional game and going along with my boyfriend's mum. It felt like a milestone in my relationship with Wayne.

*

A while later, the England team were doing a training camp in La Manga, Spain, leading up to a tournament. Wayne invited me to go with him, and Mum and Dad agreed I could. I was doing my AS-level exams at the time, so I couldn't fly with him as I had an exam that day. I had to fly out the morning after.

I was apprehensive about travelling out there alone; it felt like such a big thing. Still, Wayne was there to meet me at the airport with an FA liaison, and off we went to the hotel. Once settled, I started to get changed, ready to head down to the pool, where some other players and their wives and girlfriends were hanging out. As you can imagine, this was a fairly nerve-wracking scenario for me, picturing all these mature, glamorous and worldly people I'd never met before, especially when I'd been sitting at a school desk taking an exam the day before. Just as we were heading downstairs, Wayne dropped the bombshell.

'Right, I'm off to play golf now.'

'What? What do you mean you're playing golf? I've just got here.'

'Col, it's Michael Owen and some of the other lads; I can't not go if I've got the chance.'

It dawned on me that this was all as new to Wayne as it was to me, and he was as excited as I was.

'Well, what am I going to do while you're playing golf with Michael Owen?'

'Don't stress. I'll take you down the pool and you can meet some of the other girls,' he said.

We headed down to the pool where Wayne left me with a few other players and their partners. I sat down with them but felt extremely awkward. I didn't even know their names at the time. What the hell was I supposed to talk about? It was fine in the end, they were all very friendly.

When he came back later that day, I said, 'Well, you've played your golf now; you don't need to go off and do that again while I'm here, do you?'

I enjoyed the rest of the trip, but it's funny to think back on how young we both were. We couldn't even drink alcohol while we were there. Mind you, at the team barbecue, when the players had some downtime, one of the lads offered to go to the bar and sneak us a bevvy or two – although we made sure it was something that could be disguised as non-alcoholic, just in case.

I suppose that trip was my first real contact with any of the other players and their partners, and, in the end, it was fine. I got on well with Alex Curran, a fellow Scouser, and Wayne and I spent time with her and her partner, Steven Gerrard, a few times. I was conscious of how young we both were, but at the same time, I think I handled it well. Deep down, I knew I'd be OK if I just took things in my stride. Although that wasn't always as easy as it sounded.

*

Mum and Dad were understandably protective of me at that time. Not overly so, but they were careful. I was their eldest, but still in my mid-teens when Wayne's career took off, and being his girlfriend, they could see me being swept along with it. Looking back, I'm surprised by some of the things my parents allowed me to do at that age, and I told them as much recently.

'You were in a situation where you had to grow up fast, but I knew you were sensible.'

That was Dad's take on it, but I'm sure I wasn't always sensible; I definitely made mistakes – we both did. In many ways, he was right, though. We had no choice but to grow up fast, especially Wayne. He was thrust into an adult environment, and, as you all know, football isn't just a game; it's a serious business. There was suddenly a lot riding on Wayne, a lot of expectation and pressure on his young shoulders and, consequently, a few sacrifices to be made. Playing in the first team every weekend and all the training that went with it meant there was not much of a social life. There was also the media attention and sudden loss of privacy to contend with. Plenty of people were made up for Wayne and his success at such a young age, but there were also those who were watching his every step, just waiting for him to screw up or put a foot wrong.

Seventeen seems very young to get engaged, but that's what happened with us. We were in love, and Wayne was always one to get things moving as quickly as possible. Once he made his mind up about something, that was it.

It wasn't long after we'd started dating when I got a phone call from his cousin while I was doing homework in my bedroom.

'Coleen, do you spell your name with one L or two?' he asked.

'One,' I said. 'Why?'

'Oh, nothing, I'm just with our Wayne, and he's getting a tattoo.'

'No, he's not.' I didn't believe it for a second.

That night, I turned up at our friend's eighteenth birthday party, and Wayne was already there. I could see him working the room, pulling his sleeve up and showing everyone this bloody tattoo of my name on his shoulder. I couldn't believe he'd done it, but his thinking was that we were going to be together. There was no question in his mind, so he decided on a permanent statement.

By the time he proposed, I'd had an inkling it might happen – not the actual date and time, but I thought it might be on the cards. Wayne was never very good at keeping things under wraps or containing his excitement about something. He'd already told me he was having a ring made especially for me; I just wasn't sure it was an engagement ring.

On the night it happened, 1 October 2003, he'd planned a date at a Chinese restaurant – nothing special, it was just local to where we lived. On the way there in the car, we started bickering over something – I can't even remember what now, but whatever it was must have put me in a bit of a mood. As we pulled in at a petrol station, I folded my arms and sighed.

'Do you know? I don't really feel like going for something to eat now.'

'No, neither do I,' Wayne said, turning off the car engine. 'Only, the thing is, while we were there, I was going to do this . . .'

Then he pulled out a diamond engagement ring – right there in the petrol station.

'Oh my word!'

'Yeah,' he said.

He couldn't get down on one knee, of course – there's not really the room in a car footwell – but before I knew it, I had an emerald-cut diamond ring on my finger, and I rang my mum and dad to tell them our big news. Little did I know, he'd already asked my dad's permission, so they knew it was coming.

By the time we arrived back, Mum had lit a few candles and opened a bottle of champagne. Our engagement tea was a plate of Mum's corned-beef hash, which she'd been cooking for the family tea – simple but delicious.

All in all, it wasn't the most romantic of proposals, I'll give you that, plus I kind of expected it. What I hadn't expected was for Wayne to pop the question under the lights of an Esso garage; it's not the image a girl conjures up when she thinks about a marriage proposal, as a rule. So, in the end, I suppose you could say that at least there was still some element of surprise.

Later the same month, Wayne turned eighteen, and his mum and his agent organised a birthday party for him in conjunction with *OK!* magazine. This was a whole new experience for Wayne and me, with invitations going out to celebrities Wayne didn't even know, just for the coverage. That kind of thing seemed to happen a lot back then with magazines, but it wasn't something Wayne and I had planned on, and we haven't done it since. Walking around that night, I spotted various *Eastenders* cast members, some music business people, and a few other familiar faces. I remember thinking how weird it was for people to go to the birthday party of someone they didn't even know.

I think that's when it really started to dawn on me how big this all was, how interested people were in the person I was engaged to marry. This cheeky lad I used to see standing outside the newsagents next door to our house was fast becoming a world-famous footballer. Not only that, but they were also interested in me, and that interest grew and grew as time went on.

I didn't know it then, but the celebrity life I was stepping into would bring me so many wonderful opportunities – and a fair amount of pain.

Chapter Five

Over the years, people have asked me how I felt about being in the background, the girlfriend or wife of someone famous. The truth is, it's never fazed me. I *was* Wayne's girlfriend, the girlfriend of a premier league player. That's the reason I was in the public eye. Perhaps if I'd continued on my path with dancing in performing arts, I'd have been well-known in my own right, but we'll never know because I never took it to the next stage. I was and always have been comfortable with that fact.

With all that said, I was very blessed with everything that came my way. I didn't have to go looking for it; people came to me with ideas and opportunities, many of which I was happy to embrace. Suddenly, there were TV shows and magazines, all interested in what I was wearing or what I had to say about something. It was rare for a talent like Wayne's to come through at such a young age; therefore, his equally young girlfriend was of interest by association. 'What are they up to?' 'What do they do in their spare time?' 'What is she like?' 'What is she wearing?'

I was still at school while all this was going on – in the sixth form. As exciting as it all felt, there's no doubt that we had to grow up fast. While our relationship seemed very normal to us, to the wider world and the public it was becoming a big thing, and everybody seemed to want to know the ins and outs of everything. With that in mind, we sat down with Mick, who was part of the team at Wayne's agency and had worked with Wayne and his family for some time.

'Things could get out of control if you're not careful,' Mick told us. 'You need to be sure which direction you want to take.'

Mick explained how the press worked and how careful we had to be with what we said and did publicly. It was basic-ally a guideline on the pros and cons of life in the public eye – if that's what we wanted. As Wayne's girlfriend, I could keep my head down and not accept anything that came my way, or I could embrace what was happening and get someone to manage things properly.

Of course, this wasn't something I'd ever had to con-sider, and it was a lot to think about. I could see that what Mick said made sense with everything happening so fast, but I was still at school, just into my second year of A levels. I wasn't enjoying it, though. It was nothing to do with the school or the other pupils, it was more that I'd always strived to give it my best, to work hard and get good grades. Now I felt I wasn't fully committed. I suppose I'd seen a different side of life by then, an alternative. As time passed, more and more things were coming up for Wayne that I had the chance to be a part of – a trip abroad, an awards ceremony in London. Being part of these things meant missing school and falling behind, and that's what started to happen. Ultimately, the perfectionist in me told me I had to choose. I couldn't have both. I'd enjoyed my education until then, but suddenly there was another option. My head had been turned, so my heart wasn't in it anymore.

I sat down for a talk with Mum and Dad, who were concerned but supportive, and then I did the same with Wayne. At the end of all that, I decided I wanted to leave school and take up some of the offers coming my way. It wasn't something I did lightly. A big part of me felt disappointed in myself for not seeing it through. My teachers weren't on board with the decision either, some telling my parents I'd made the wrong call. I wasn't surprised; I'd had a good relationship with them. They saw me as a good student, a hard worker with a lot of potential. At the same time, I knew I wouldn't get the grades I needed to take me on to the next step and to a good university. Plus, I could always change my mind and return to education if I wanted. My mind was made up.

From that point on, life seemed to open up. Wayne was working a lot, but when he wasn't, we were free to enjoy time with one another and do a few nice things together, without me worrying about homework assignments or exams. We flew to Paris one weekend, although we were followed by reporters the whole time we were there, made various day trips, and attended more events as a couple. It felt like a great time to be young and just enjoying life, so that's what we did.

With Wayne spending more and more time staying at our house, we decided to take the next step and get our own place. We were so young. When I think back on some of the big decisions I made at seventeen, it makes my head spin.

As someone attempting to run a home, Mum was a tough act to follow; she was the perfect hostess. Whoever came around to our house always got properly fed and watered. Meanwhile, I struggled to make a decent cup of tea, and my cooking skills left much to be desired. And that was just the start of it. What was I supposed to do when the window cleaners came? Should I offer them a hot drink like Mum always did? Even now, Dad gives the lads who come to spray the wheelie bins refreshments in the garden. I wasn't sure if I should be knocking up rounds of butties for anyone who turned up on the doorstep. I didn't think I had time to be as hospitable as my parents always were. And what about the house itself – decorating? Gardening?

Thankfully, we had plenty of good people around us to advise us on all that stuff. When you're a premier league footballer signed to a major agency, they'll take on a lot of day-to-day stuff for you. We had people advising us and

sorting things out on our behalf as far as the house went –
and thank heavens, because that gave us time to find our
feet with it all.

That said, we were both very grounded. We'd come
from families where everyone worked hard and did everything for themselves. We knew what it took to get through
life, even if we hadn't yet gotten to grips with how to negotiate it daily. I didn't want everything done for me, and I
never expected it either.

Although our new house was in Formby, just half an
hour from Mum and Dad's place, it might as well have
been ten hours away. That's how it felt being so far away
from my family.

With Wayne playing matches away every other week,
I never wanted to stay in the house alone. I'd either pack
a bag and head off to Mum and Dad's or get one of my
brothers or friends over. They were still at school but could
stay over on weekends when Wayne was playing.

The realisation that I'd moved from my family home –
that warm, wonderful, safe environment – brought up so
much emotion in me that I found it hard to deal with. At
times, I'd even get teary when I drove from my mum's
place back to Formby. Despite everything that was going
on around me, I still sometimes felt like a kid playing house.
I kept having to remind myself how protective my parents
had always been, and if they hadn't thought I could cope,
they wouldn't have let me do it. I was sensible, wasn't I?

I had a good head on my shoulders. Surely, if they could trust in me, I could trust in myself.

The summer of 2004 started fairly well; we had a couple of exciting trips planned and there was the European Championships in Portugal to look forward to. Unfortunately, that tournament didn't end well when Wayne tangled with Portuguese defender Jorge Andrade and ended up with a broken foot.

It was only twenty or so minutes into the match, and that was it; he was gone. I'd been watching it all with my heart in my mouth then, finally, his agent came and said Wayne was being taken to hospital. Wayne later told me that in the hospital there were TVs everywhere, all tuned to the match. He'd had to watch the rest of the game and the penalty shoot-out, which England ultimately lost, in agony and gutted that he wasn't still on the pitch.

After the drama of all that, we flew to New York for the start of our holiday, but with all the publicity surrounding Wayne, plus a broken foot, his agent Paul suggested we take security. Neither of us were keen, but we agreed to take a guy called Damian, who worked for Manchester United.

As it turned out, we were glad of Damian in New York – it was busy and there were a lot of press and paparazzi around. For the second phase of our holiday, however, in Barbados, there wasn't much for him to do at all. Poor

Damian ended up being our personal photographer as well as my partner for beach and water activities. Wayne's never been a big fan of water and swimming anyway, but with a broken foot, he couldn't do anything. So, while he sat on the back of a boat, Damian and I would be speeding along behind on a rubber ring or water skis.

All in all, the trip was wonderful, but when we flew home to the UK, it was straight into another fast-gathering storm.

Still freshly tanned by the Barbadian sun, we were back at home in Formby and I noticed Wayne was acting strangely, as if he were building himself up to tell me something. When the storm finally broke, it was a mighty one.

During the time we'd dated, there had been the odd bit of gossip about Wayne being up to no good in the past, visiting massage parlours with his mates. While it bothered me to hear, it was, as far as I was concerned, just gossip. Only it wasn't.

It turned out that when he'd started rising through the ranks at Everton, he was a lad with a few extra pounds in his pocket, acting a bit cocky. His mates from the area were nice enough lads, but they were getting up to stuff they shouldn't have. Not that anyone else was to blame – it seems to me that Wayne played his part, trying to be the big man with some of the boys he was knocking around with.

The full story was that when he was sixteen, Wayne had

visited prostitutes in a Liverpool massage parlour. When Wayne sat me down and told me it was true and that the story was about to break in the national press, I was confused and hurt. I couldn't even speak to him. More than that, I felt ashamed. Mum and Dad were away at the time, on holiday in Florida with Rosie and Anthony. How the hell was I supposed to pick up the phone and tell them what had happened? I didn't think I'd even be able to find the right words. Instead, I drove to Mum and Dad's empty house, where I sat, crying in my bedroom; turning things over in my mind but not getting anywhere. In the end, I called Dad's sister, my auntie Tracy, who told me to come round to her house. I stayed with her that night, and we talked it through, trying to understand why Wayne had felt the need to do something like that when he already had me. I had no idea what I would do or how to move forward. By then, I was used to seeing stories in the press that involved me – the odd candid, intrusive paparazzi shot – but this was on another level. How was I supposed to deal with something as awful as this?

'I need to tell Mum and Dad before it comes out in the paper,' I told Tracy. 'I can't bear the thought of them finding out like that.'

Tracy called Mum and Dad for me to let them know what was going on, and then we spoke to my grandparents. I didn't feel like talking to anyone else, but I had to warn my close family.

Mum and Dad were angry, and I understood their anger. Dad has always been a good listener, keen to weigh up a situation. I think in that way, I'm very like him; I'm a big-picture person. Their first instinct was to protect me as their little girl, and they felt gutted that they couldn't be there to help me through it. Still, I knew they were always there on the end of the phone, and if they couldn't be there, they knew Auntie Tracy would look after me while they were away. There have been times over the years when it's been hard for my parents, with various stories coming out in the press. They're proud, good people who feel pain, knowing something is hurting or affecting their child. For that reason, my decisions regarding Wayne haven't always been what they've thought best, but they trust me to know. They know that whatever happens, I'll have thought it all through and done what's best for my family, for my kids, and they've always supported that. Still, I have felt for them over the years, having to deal with it.

After the story broke, it was no longer something we could just deal with as a family. Suddenly, our house in Formby was swamped with press. There were reporters and photographers everywhere we turned. Everyone knew, and everyone seemed to have an opinion. I sat with it all swirling around me like some horrible dream, unable to decide what was best or even what I wanted. A voice inside me told me not to do anything rash, not to make a decision in the midst of my anger. Dealing with that kind of thing was heart-breaking enough, but I was eighteen years old. I was upset and confused, not knowing what to think or how others might react. I wasn't sure what I felt about Wayne anymore. Also, I knew my family's instinct would be to protect me, and whatever way you spun it, this was not a good look.

Tracy suggested I talk to Wayne. I knew she was right; I had to. Wayne had told me there was some truth to the story, but I still didn't know all the details and circumstances. I had to hear it all from his lips.

I let several days pass before I sat down with him to talk. I wanted to have my thoughts together. He ended up coming to Tracy and Shaun's, so we could try to work things out. After a few days of talking, he came and stayed there with me. Apart from our closest family, no one knew we were there. Every morning, Wayne would get up and travel to his training, hiding in the back of Shaun's little white van to avoid any press who might be on the look out for us while we were still working things out. He'd travel back home the same way, with Shaun taking a different route every day.

Wayne admitted the story was true but told me some of it had been fabricated for effect. It had happened a couple of years before, but it probably wouldn't have been news if the story had come out then. Now, Wayne was on the England squad, playing for his country, so the story packed a punch.

I'd been sixteen when Wayne had gone to the massage parlour. I'd started going out with him that August and it happened over the Christmas period, a few months into our relationship. I'm not sure I'd say it was even a proper relationship at that stage – we were such babies. I certainly hadn't slept with him.

Once we were talking again, Tracy and Shaun suggested we experience some normality and get ourselves out of the house for a bit. We ended up going for a bite to eat, and then walked around a few shops in Manchester where, thankfully, nobody spotted us. A few evenings later, we went to Blackpool Pleasure Beach, both wearing hats with our collars turned up. Again, we weren't recognised apart from a flicker from the odd passer-by. It was a calm and lovely evening, and we were just a young couple at the seaside. Free to be ourselves and to talk honestly about our feelings.

He knew how bad this was, how wrong. He looked down at the floor as he told me how devastated he felt having put me in that situation. I was still fuming, of course, and there were definitely a few screaming matches in the days to come. In the end, though, I accepted that this had happened a long time ago and that we were stronger now, more committed. We weren't the kids we were back then, and Wayne was no longer the cocky lad trying to impress his mates. If I'd found out he was having an affair or he'd told me he was in love with someone else, I couldn't have gotten over it, but that wasn't the case.

I couldn't have known it then, but I'd be tested like this again in the future, more than once. I say the same thing now as I did back then. If you're dealing with something stupid done in the heat of the moment involving alcohol, it might be fixable. If love, emotions and ongoing deception are involved, then it's a different story. It's never right and never acceptable, but there are ways of getting through things if that's what you want and someone means that much to you.

Still, there's been lasting damage from all of that. There's been a mark on Wayne from the day that story broke. Certain areas of the press have never let up, and it's somehow been woven into the Wayne Rooney brand. Even when something good happens, something unrelated, some journalists will always find a way to remind people within the story what Wayne did when he was sixteen. Yes, he did something wrong when he was a normal young kid in an abnormal situation, and I've never said that's OK, but we've moved on with our lives. I sometimes wish other people would. I'm writing about it now because it's my side of the story from my perspective. It's what happened rather than what everyone thinks happened.

It's easy to look at these situations as an outsider and say, 'Oh, look, she's taken him back, and it's all fine,' but with me, it's never as simple as that. People might see a picture of us happily reunited after we've been through difficulties in our marriage, but they don't know what we've been through to get to that one smiling snapshot. Sometimes, it's been hard and sometimes, even when we're smiling, things might not be perfect. It's never a simple case of forgive and forget because you don't forget. Those ups and downs become part of your history as a couple, and you deal with them in the best way you can. If it's something you think you can never get over, then there isn't any point in going on. I'm glad to say that hasn't been the case for me.

Alcohol has a lot to answer for; as far as Wayne is concerned, it's often been his downfall. Often, when something is bothering Wayne, he bottles it up. Instead of coming out with the thing that's bothering him, relieving himself of the burden, he pushes it down. Then, sometimes, he'll go off on one, behaving in a way that makes everything worse. He's done it several times over the years, going out and getting drunk, and sometimes I hardly recognise him. I sometimes ask myself if he should drink at all, but in a normal situation, when we're having a few drinks with friends, he's no different to anyone else. We have a nice time.

There are times, though, when things have gone awry, and he can't control his drinking, and it's generally when something is going on in life that he can't deal with. That's when he makes bad decisions and doesn't know what he's doing or why he's doing it. He doesn't wake up in the morning craving a drink, or get violent. This is more like binges when he's trying to drown something out. Wayne is loving, affectionate, and not afraid to show it, but if something worries him, he goes dark. He doesn't share his problems; he pushes them down until they can't be pushed any further, and then they explode and he'll go on a bender.

For me, it's like walking a tightrope. That thin line between alcohol as a fun, social thing and something destructive has been the most challenging part of our relationship. This was the first time something like that happened between us, but it wouldn't be the last.

Around the same time as the grim massage parlour press story, we faced another big challenge – Wayne's transfer from Everton to play for Manchester United. It was a tough decision all round. Everton was his team; it was the local team. His family are big blues, Everton through and through.

We all know the rivalry between Manchester and Liverpool football clubs, so a lifelong Everton supporter, and now player, transferring to a Manchester team was big news. For many people, it was wrong, plain and simple. A Liverpool lad, a Scouser, playing for the rival city was seen as traitorous. He shouldn't be going there.

For Wayne, it was a chance to move forward. He was keen to play under Sir Alex Ferguson, who he saw as a fantastic manager, and wanted to win tournaments and trophies, which is what Man United was doing so well then. It's what he felt he was made for and why he got into playing in the first place.

I was proud that he took the plunge and decided to go, that he didn't listen to all the voices calling for his head. But there was a backlash, which came swiftly.

We came home one day to find 'Judas' spray painted across the wall outside our house and on a wall near my mum's place. We couldn't even go out to a bar in Liverpool without someone shouting something nasty at us. It was bitterly hard for Wayne, and those words cut deeply.

'Manc Bastard!'

'Traitor!'

Of course, it was just a minority, but aren't they always the ones with the loudest voices? It got to the stage where he stopped going out in Liverpool altogether.

On the other side of the coin, our friends, family and close circle knew the score and totally understood and respected Wayne's decision.

Still, his controversial move, coupled with the recent scandal, meant that we found ourselves all over the papers – a front- and back-page couple – and suddenly, everyone had an opinion. When you're in the midst of something like that, it's hard to see the light at the end of the tunnel. I felt like Wayne was public enemy number one and, by association, maybe I was too.

Sir Alex told Wayne he didn't want him staying at the

house anymore and that we should stay at a hotel until we could sort something permanent in Manchester. It wasn't merely a safety issue; he felt Wayne should be closer to the training ground and, in some ways, experience a different life from the one he'd known. He assured us he would do the best for us and that we should ask him if we ever needed any help. Maybe Sir Alex was right. Maybe it was time for a new start.

Wayne made his debut at Old Trafford in September 2004, in a Champions League game against Turkish side Fenerbahce, wearing the number 8 shirt. Like most Champions League games, it was at night. I went along with my dad, uncle, brothers and Claire. For some reason, that night I'd gone for bright yellow moon boots as my chosen footwear. The subsequent paparazzi picture followed me for a long time. Still, in my defence, they were very in at the time – well, I thought they were. Still, whenever I get asked now what my biggest fashion faux pas was, I always answer, 'Those yellow moon boots!' It was the first time I'd worn them and probably the last, although I've still got them.

It was an exciting night. Wayne scored a hat-trick, which was unbelievable. Not only his first Man United game but his first Champions League game as well. We all screamed as that third goal went in – he was the youngest player ever to score a hat-trick in the Champions League, and on his debut too. I felt so proud of him, knowing he'd made the right decision with the transfer. I remember thinking, *Wow! What an exciting journey he's got ahead of him.*

Suddenly, all the bad stuff we'd gone through, the taunts, the snide remarks and the graffiti on the wall, felt like a distant memory.

For us, moving to Cheshire had been a massive deal. Liverpool was our home; it's where we'd been born and grown up. It was all we'd known. We moved to a rented house there and bought a plot of land for a new house in Prestbury that was in the planning stage but not yet built.

As expected, the press interest around our new house was off the charts. Speculation about what fixtures and fittings were going into the so-called 'Rooney Mansion' got ridiculous – a tanning booth, a gold swimming pool; this list went on. The truth was, nobody knew what we were doing, and it certainly wasn't that.

Adjacent to the back of our house was a housing complex, and before we moved in, we got a few requests to cut down some trees blocking sunlight from those houses' gardens. While we were dealing with all that, Paul started getting newspapers calling him, saying they'd been given stories about the house and wanted confirmation on their accuracy. After a bit of digging, we found out that someone in the housing complex had been renting a room to a journalist whose sole purpose was to spy on the house and report on everything happening. I have no idea what explosive details he was expecting to get, given it was just

the back of the house in his sights, but it was the closest he could get. I wondered what sort of person would
rent their room to someone who wanted to spy on us and
report their findings, but I guess some people would do
anything for money. It's taking the nosy neighbours thing
to a whole new level.

During construction, I was introduced to interior
designer Dawn Ward, whose company was building the
house. Dawn was one of my first friends in the area, intro-
ducing me to a few other girls, showing me around, and
helping me make friends and connections.

It was our first real taste of the place Wayne and I
would soon call home, and we both realised this would
be a whole new chapter. Striding out on our own, much
further away from our families, meant we both had some
growing up to do.

I was excited about the prospect of moving into that
house. It had been a massive project for such a young
couple to take on, but I felt proud that we'd had a hand in
designing and building it from the bottom up. The fact that
we finally moved in on 16 December 2005, a week before
Christmas, was perfect. A brand-new start, and somewhere
we'd spend a considerable chunk of our lives – sixteen
years – with incredible highs and a few terrible lows.

Chapter Six

When I look back now, I realise how hard it was for Wayne in the early days of his career. I remember him trying to get through press interviews, not knowing how to act sometimes, or being scared of saying the wrong thing to the wrong person. These days, more players are coming through at a young age, and they're prepared for it properly. Back then, it was almost unheard of for someone to play at that level so young. Consequently, Wayne had no media training or preparation before being sent in front of the cameras.

There were all the stories assuming he couldn't read or write. He was a boy from a rough council estate who never finished school and was, therefore, stupid. This was the label hung around his neck, that myth that's always stuck, and it was so frustrating to witness.

I put up with similar assumptions and labels – the shopaholic, the chav made good, the ultimate WAG. When I was first in the public eye, plenty of magazines shamed celebrities for the size of their thighs or how they looked in a bikini. Great big red ticks and crosses across various women on a magazine cover – she looks fine, but look at this one, she looks shit! She's got cellulite – shock, horror! That was the media at the time, and thankfully, to a large extent, it's changed with all kinds of body-shapes appearing in the likes of *Vogue*, *Cosmopolitan* and other magazines. Don't get me wrong, it's still lurking in some dark corners and certain columns; it's just not as full-out evident. The more we can do to make it disappear, the better. Recently, I saw a clip of a beautiful and curvy swimsuit model walking the catwalk at designer Melissa Odabash's show, and I thought, *Yes! We've come a long way*. It's a shame there's no stricter regulation on how people talk to one another on social media – the cruel insults and the trolling. That's the issue these days.

I've always been a relatively strong person, so, on the whole, I didn't let that stuff get to me back in the day. Even when it did bother me, it wasn't for long. I'd get upset by the odd nasty comment, but I was able to shake it off fairly quickly. There were plenty of good things alongside all that, so I tried to concentrate on those. If I had gone down the rabbit hole of letting the negative stuff affect me, I don't think I could have taken on the projects I did on TV and in magazines.

I sometimes wish Wayne had been more like me in that respect and had more confidence in himself off the pitch. Whatever scrutiny I was under, he had tenfold.

One thing I've never done is put on a show for the press. I've never once organised or set up a paparazzi shot.

I'm not knocking people who do; sometimes, it's a publicity thing that can work well, and sometimes I've known people who'll agree to split any money the shot makes with the photographer. Fair play to them.

To be honest, I've never had to set up shots anyway because, good or bad, photographers tend to turn up without any help from me. Plus, if you make that arrangement once, you're stuck with it. You can't court the press when you're all dolled up to the nines and it suits you, then moan about it when you're snapped coming out of Waitrose in a tracky with your hair dragged back in a ponytail. You can't have it both ways.

Having my picture taken is something I've become very accustomed to over the years. Most of the time, I let it wash over me. There are days when I'll stop and say to a photographer, 'Come on, mate, every day you take a picture of me coming out of a coffee shop. Why do you need another one?'

On other days, I'll just put my head down and go straight to the car without looking up. It just depends on what kind of mood I'm in on a particular day. I've long given up worrying about my appearance when I get papped on a typical morning. OK, so there are days when I think, *Oh no, my hair. Why did I come out with my hair looking such a show?* But if I had to worry about being camera ready every time I dashed out to do the school or supermarket run, I'd never get out of the friggin' house. There's a big contrast between those shots and those where I'm photographed at an event, having had a decent blow-dry and my make-up done, but I guess that's real life, isn't it? So, if I don't look a hundred per cent all the time, that's just me. I don't know how else to be.

As for online comments, I tend to avoid reading them. I used to. I used to read all of them and take them in, good and bad. Sometimes they were just pure hatred, and I'd think, *What have these people got against me? They don't know me, and I've not done anything to them, so why do they hate me?* I remember seeing comments where I was described as 'a little stump' due to my petite stature, or people making nasty comments about the prominent mole I have on the side of my face. 'The little stump with the massive mole!'

I'm pretty strong-minded. Yes, I know I'm only short, and I know I have a mole on my face, but there's nothing I can do to change it, and I wouldn't want to anyway. So, why worry about what some anonymous person hiding behind a keyboard thinks? There were times when I was younger when it was a little more challenging, but these days, I can let it wash over me.

I'm grateful for that strength but not everyone has it. We've all seen how living under the spotlight from a young age and relentless media attention can affect some celebrities. Take someone like Britney Spears, who suffered constant negativity for a long time, as troubled as she was. Even when she reached a crisis point, the circus continued, and the press stories perpetuated more public attention, eventually breaking her.

I think you have to be made of strong stuff to live life in the public eye, and those who aren't can sometimes go off the rails. A person who becomes famous for their talent might otherwise be perfectly ordinary, with the same insecurities and flaws as the next person. Being famous doesn't necessarily give you the tools to withstand all that goes along with that fame.

I'll admit there are still times when it affects me, particularly when it comes to my marriage, but these days it's more frustrating than upsetting. Imagine watching a group of people on a morning TV show, all giving their opinions about the state of your love life when they only have a fraction of the information. I've often imagined picking up the phone to a person and asking, 'What's going on in your life that makes you so down on people you don't even know?' In fact, in the past, I did exactly that.

Not long after Wayne and I moved to Manchester, there was a double-page spread about me in the *Daily Mail*, which was nothing less than vulgar. The journalist left no stone unturned in his disdain for me, my lifestyle, my family, my relationship and my very existence. It was hideous and really knocked me for six. I remember feeling helpless and without a voice. It was frustrating to think that somebody could write these things about me without a second thought about who I was or what it might do to me. I was eighteen – a baby. How dare he?

Sitting in our newly rented home in Wilmslow, I called

the *Daily Mail* and asked to speak to the journalist who'd penned this hatchet job.

After a few minutes on the switchboard, getting passed around the building, he was finally on the other end of the phone line.

'Can I ask you a question? Do you know me?' I asked him.

'I'm sorry?'

'Do you know me personally?'

'I don't understand.'

'This is Coleen McLoughlin, and you have just written a two-page spread about me, my relationship and my family, so I'm thinking you must know me.'

'Well, I . . .'

'Exactly, you haven't got a clue.' I'm pretty sure the guy hadn't factored this into his day. 'Have you got any kids? Because I'm someone's daughter. Do you think it's OK for my mum and dad to pick up your paper and read that about me, their daughter? Because it's not. It's not nice, and it's not right.'

I could hear him breathing on the other end of the line, not knowing what to say for himself. In the end, he fudged a reply, something about just doing his job.

'Fair enough,' I said. 'Then do your research a bit more thoroughly. Write the truth. I'm a person with feelings, and the person you've written about is the opposite of who I am.'

For the next couple of years, we seemed to be living from one crazy press story to the next. I went through this period where photographers would turn up everywhere I went. Not just the obvious places when it was something to do with a football game or an event – this was everywhere. I remember one day driving to a friend's house in Croxteth. It was down a street you'd never pass unless you had to, and I'd only popped in for a minute. When I came out, there was a pap snapping pictures of me. It struck me as a bit weird at the time, but then it kept happening. I'd be running to the shops or round to my mum's, and there they were. I couldn't seem to go anywhere without a photographer in tow, and it really started to unnerve me. Eventually, we hired an investigator through a security firm we'd previously worked with.

When I was leaving the gym one morning, the investigator came and told me he'd caught someone putting something under my car. It turned out to be a tracker, which needed a change of batteries every few days. That morning, the investigator had caught someone changing one tracker for another. Heaven knows how long the bloody thing had been there, but now, at last, the mystery was solved. The culprit was from a London-based firm employed to get content for various newspapers, and I was his chosen target.

My friends and I tried to think up various ways to avoid being photographed or to trick the press. We usually came up with silly little plots, but we got a buzz out of putting them into action. When Claire and I drove to visit Louise at her mum's one day, with photographers in tow as usual, we decided it might be funny if we swapped clothes. After the visit, Claire came out in the outfit I'd gone inside wearing, got in my car, and drove away. Sure enough, the press followed her and I was able to slip out without being tailed for once. I also took convoluted routes and shortcuts walking around Alderley Edge if someone spotted me. I knew the area well, so I'd often lose them, then get back to my car and away before they managed to catch me. It didn't always work, but when it did, I got a good laugh out of it, relishing each small victory.

Still, there were times when it got too much, and I lost the battle. My first proper girls' holiday was to Tenerife with Claire and Louise – or Brenda as she's affectionately known. I'd planned to go to Magaluf in Spain with a group of girls earlier that summer. Still, I was worried the press attention I'd get might screw up their holiday, so I bowed out. As it turned out, it was probably the right decision.

While Claire, Louise and I were away, we hung out at Linekers in Playa de las Americas, which is quite famous and well-known for its lively atmosphere. While we were there one night, everyone was doing this mad worm dance to the song 'The Lion Sleeps Tonight'. It's like the flow of a Mexican wave, with everyone joining hands. Anyway, there I am doing the dance, innocently linking hands with the person next to me, who just happened to be one of Linekers' topless barmen. A photo was taken, and the following day, a cropped version appeared on the front pages of a newspaper back in the UK, with a story about me flirting with a half-naked mystery man.

Wayne, who was away with the England team at the time, phoned me to ask what the bloody hell I was up to.

'I've got nothing to explain; it was a cropped photo,' I told him. 'I've done nothing.'

I got very upset after the call, but Claire and Louise kept reminding me that we all knew the truth and that I'd done nothing to feel guilty about.

There were also pictures taken at our hotel which appeared in the UK papers, but we had no idea who was taking them as there were no press photographers around – well, none that we could see anyway. It all got quite wearing; still, we did our best to enjoy the holiday and tried not to think about it.

A couple of nights before the cropped photo incident, we were out at a club, dancing the night away with a couple of other girls we knew, Faye and Sinead, who were out there with their families. While we were happily enjoying ourselves, some local girls started jostling us and giving us the evil eye. Eventually, one of them shoved Claire off the raised podium section we were dancing on. Claire retaliated, but because the Spanish girls were known to the club's security, it was Claire who got marched out of the club.

I stuck with Faye and Sinead on Louise's orders while she stalked off to find out what had happened to Claire. When she got outside, she was horrified to see one of these girls punching Claire while Claire slid down a wall. Louise ran across to intervene, but then one of the girls grabbed her and she got punched too. As the girls ran off, cackling and victorious, Claire and Louise found themselves lying on the floor, dazed and confused and wondering what the hell had happened. How had a simple girls' night out gone so horribly wrong?

Eventually, I made my way out of the club under the rock-solid protection of Faye and Sinead. Then Louise, Claire and I made our way back to our hotel, all wishing we'd never bothered to leave it.

When we woke up the following morning, all in the same hotel room, Louise had a massive coggie on her forehead. Not the best holiday look, I'm sure you'll agree. We spent the morning trying to piece together the previous night's events, but by then, I was convinced the holiday had been a bad idea. Cursed from the off.

The final straw came when we went into town for a spot of quiet shopping, but even then, photographers followed us. When a man came bobbing out of nowhere and asked if he could have his photograph taken with me, I politely told him I couldn't do that because of all the press

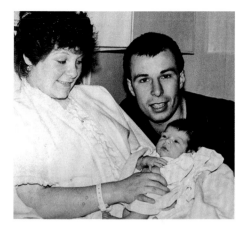

Where it all began: my mum, Colette, and dad, Tony, holding me in the hospital on the day I was born, 3 April 1986.

Dressed up and ready to celebrate my Christening Day.

All ready for my First Holy Communion ceremony.

My mum surrounded by me, my brothers Joe and Anthony and my cousin Clair.

Toddler Wayne and his trademark cheeky grin.

Me on my summer holidays in Spain.

Me, Joe, Anthony and our beautiful Rosie at Christmas in our family home in Croxteth.

Wayne and my brothers Anthony (*left*) and Joe (*right*) in Barbados.

All smiles outside the family home on the first day of the school year.

Summer lovin': me, Joe and Anthony with our dad on holiday in Florida in June 1998.

Teenage kicks: celebrating my eighteenth birthday.

And celebrating Wayne's eighteenth birthday together.

Rosie, me and Dad at our family home.

Getting ready for dinner with Rosie in Dubai.

Jeans for Genes: raising awareness for Jeans for
Genes Day 2014, where I regularly participated
as a panellist for the charity T-shirt design
competition to raise awareness for people living
with genetic conditions like my sister Rosie.

Together at a Robbie Williams concert.

Young love: Wayne and me in the early years of our relationship.

At the opening of a new neuro unit at the Alder Hey Children's Hospital in our home city of Liverpool in 2006.

Alder Hey is one of the biggest and busiest children's hospitals in Europe and is where they took great care of my sister Rosie. Wayne, the family and I have continued to support Alder Hey ever since.

(*Above*) Preparing for my first book signing.
(*Left*) At a signing for my very first
autobiography, *Coleen: Welcome to My World*
in 2007.

All aboard: with Mum and my
sisters-in-law Carley and Amy
on a barge we hired for the
weekend.

Unlikely celebrations: me,
my best friends and Mum
celebrating my birthday in my
parents' garden in the lead up
to the trial in 2022.

(*Above*) me, my nan, my auntie Ellie and Kai in Portugal. (*Below*) My grandparents Dolly and Tommy with Kai.

Fairy-tale wedding, as photographed by *Ok! Magazine* for our wedding in Italy in 2008.

The whole family attending Kai's Holy Communion and Cass's Christening Day.

Making memories: me, Kai, Klay and Kit on
Castaway Cay island in the Bahamas.

Wayne and me with the kids in the Bahamas.

My sister-in-law Amy, my nephew Bobby, niece Blake, Klay, Cass, Kai, Kit and me all enjoying the
sunset on the beach in Mexico.

and cameras following us around. Without another word, the guy grabbed me around the neck and tried to kiss me for the photographers.

'Get off me, get away!' I smacked him in the face with my bag, and Claire and Louise dived in to help.

Another bloody scuffle – what was this, a girl's holiday or *The Hunger Games*?

The guy grabbing me was the last straw. I was in tears, shaken up and wondering whether the whole thing had been a set-up between the man and the paparazzi. We booked a flight that day and came home, cutting our holiday short by three days. I was disappointed, and I felt terrible for Claire and Louise. They'd probably have had a lovely time if I hadn't been with them. Instead, we'd been driven off the island by the press and all the attention I was getting. I'd long ago accepted that being in the public eye meant I'd have to take the rough with the smooth, and this was definitely the rough!

Around the same time as the disastrous Tenerife holiday, Wayne got into a legal battle with the *Sun* and *News of the World* newspapers. It came about after a night out that had gone wrong and inevitably ended up in the press, but, as is often the case, the story was in part fabricated and very defamatory to Wayne.

It all started on a Sunday afternoon when we'd been invited over to Rio Ferdinand's house to watch a game and have some drinks and food with a few others from the team and their partners. It was a lovely social occasion, but the boys had a few drinks and decided to head to Brasingamens, a club in Alderley Edge, for some more. Sunday was the club's big night, they had a good DJ on, and it was always packed. None of us girls fancied it, though, and from what I could gather, the invitation didn't extend to us anyway.

'Why can't we just stay here and have a nice time?' I said to Wayne. 'I'm not up for a late night.'

I was flying to Cyprus the following day for a photo shoot to get some promo shots, so the last thing I needed was more alcohol and a late night.

The lads were determined, though, and Wayne insisted he was going too. I think a few of them just wanted to go out and do their thing without the girls in tow, so that's what they did. This lovely social Sunday had suddenly turned into a boys' night out.

Once they'd disappeared, us girls sat around feeling left out and pissed off. That was until someone said, 'Sod this, why should we stay in when they're all out clubbing?'

The next thing I knew, Rio's partner Rebecca was rooting through her wardrobe, doling out various bits of clothing to some of the other girls, while we were all glamming ourselves up, getting ready to hit the town.

When we rocked up at Brasingamens the looks on the boys' faces told us that they weren't all that thrilled to see us. Some of them were less happy than others, and

I noticed a few couples not getting on throughout the evening – mostly fuelled by too much alcohol. Wayne and I were no different, with me yelling at Wayne to come home. As heated as it got, that was the sum of it, but the story in the press the following morning was far more sinister. The *Sun* said Wayne had hit me in the face. 'Crazed Rooney Thumps Coleen' was the headline – completely untrue. A *News of the World* story with the headline 'Rooney: The Truth' said Wayne had punched me in the ribs and chest and told me to 'fuck off home' before being restrained by his teammates.

Aside from insisting this was all a lie and never happened, there were paparazzi photos of me arriving in Cyprus the next day, unmarked and looking fine. I'm pretty sure if Wayne or any man had punched me in the face, there'd have been some evidence of it, but that didn't dissuade the papers from sticking with their line, hence Wayne's legal battle with them.

By the time I got into my hotel room in Cyprus it had all kicked off because of the stories; photographers were everywhere. Press reports said I was there to do a *Vogue* photo shoot, which was incorrect; we were doing some shots to use for various upcoming projects – but that seemed to make the story about Wayne punching me even juicier. At one point, I stepped out onto the balcony to take a phone call and spotted a man on the balcony of the next room looking over at me. It was one of the pap photographers who'd been at the airport and outside the hotel – staying in the room next to mine.

I went into a panic. It was one of the first times I remember feeling scared when it came to being in the eye of the media. All sorts of things went through my mind. Would he be listening through the wall to my phone conversations? Could he climb across the balcony divide and photograph me in my room? It felt so intrusive, and I was scared and bloody angry.

I called Jane Aspinall, who worked with Paul's agency and was on the trip with me, and told her what was happening. She quickly had me moved to another room. I managed to get through the next couple of days, and we got the shots we needed. I was shaken up, though. This had started as a Sunday afternoon, just having drinks with some friends, and ended up turning into a circus.

Wayne's legal battle went on for some time, and in the end, both newspapers settled without going to court. The *Sun* paid Wayne a sum reflecting the seriousness of the libel, plus legal costs. They also had to print an apology, but, as we all know with that, the apologies are usually scraped in and tiny compared to the original story, plus, in most cases, the damage is already done.

Reflecting on all this now, it feels like so much happened over a short space of time. As things got bigger and Wayne's career really took off, there was so much to celebrate, but it all went hand in hand with the stresses and anxieties that came with all that success. We'd gone from being two fairly ordinary Scouse kids to living life under a microscope. Stories about Wayne Rooney, the footballer, had shifted from the back pages to the front pages. It was more than a game now, more than just a sport. This was our whole lives being opened up to the world, and while it was sometimes tough on me, for Wayne, who always does his best to hide from the spotlight, it was like his worst nightmare.

It's never-ending, really. In 2012, Wayne was one of many high-profile people who were part of a phone hacking case with News Group Newspapers, who ended up settling out of court. As far as I knew, my name had never come up as someone who'd been hacked. Still, during the recent court case with Rebekah Vardy, my lawyer David Sherborne asked me why I'd never put in a claim – he'd been a barrister for many of the celebrities involved in phone hacking incidents over the years.

'Why would I make a claim? As far as I know, I've never been hacked,' I said.

'Oh yes,' he said. 'Your name is on a list. I've seen it mentioned several times in connection with hacking.'

I can't say much for legal reasons at the time of writing this, but there is now a phone hacking claim in process.

I suppose I wasn't all that surprised to hear that I'd been hacked. That kind of thing has become part of our lives over the years, and we always have to be vigilant.

It might not be normal to most people, but it's just how it is.

Over the years, though, I feel I've handled myself reasonably well in the media. I've not fallen out of clubs drunk or done anything particularly outrageous in front of the cameras. Still, there is that party-girl side to me – I love a party – but I'm also a mum and a wife.

In an interview, a friend said I was a closed book, which is half true. I don't like to give too much away, but that's because of the world I've lived in for the past twenty years – where your every move is scrutinised. If I don't know someone well, I might put a bit of a guard up. If someone gets to know me well, and I trust them, I'm usually happy to open up and talk about anything and everything. Well, almost anything! I also pride myself on being a good judge of character. A couple of times over the years, my mates have said, 'Ah, she's lovely,' or 'He's good for me,' about a person, while I've remained cautious – sensing something off about them. Sure enough, down the line, the person in question has shown their true colours or done the dirty, and my mates will be back saying, 'Coleen, you called that one ages ago!'

It's a quality I have, a superpower perhaps, and I'm glad of it.

Chapter Seven

In the lead-up to the 2006 World Cup in Germany, there was a huge amount of press interest in the wives and girl-friends of some of the England players. That tournament is famously where the term WAG came into its own.

The tournament felt very exciting, and I was thrilled to be going out for all of it – well, at least as long as England stayed in.

Although the families all paid for their own travel and accommodation, this was the first time the FA had helped with organising everything. Everyone stayed in the same hotel, and transport was laid on to and from the games and various tournament events. Being together often meant that I got to know the other girls a lot better – Elen Rivas, Alex Curran, Louise Owen and Carly Zuker, to name a few. As well as Alex, who I'd already made friends with, I got to know Lisa Roughead, Michael Carrick's girl-friend, now wife, and we've been friends ever since. Claire and I also got on well with Cheryl, who was only weeks away from marrying Ashley Cole. It was a good crowd of

girls, and as a bit more camaraderie developed, we naturally started socialising together along with all our families.

Baden-Baden, where we were staying, is a smart spa
town on the edge of the Black Forest, boasting a handful
of restaurants and one late bar. I don't know what it's like
now, but it wasn't exactly the Las Vegas strip back then. Of
course, we all went out and had fun, but the stories about
us going crazy and running riot were wildly exaggerated.

Because it was so small and everyone was in one place,
it was easy for the press to congregate and get plenty of
photographs. If we'd been in Lisbon, for example, spread
out all over the city, they'd never have gotten that amount
of content. In Baden-Baden, even if we hadn't gone out
together one night, we'd all end up at the same place
because there were so few places to end up. There were
fans amongst us at the bar and, of course, there was enthusiasm and singing with everyone getting behind England.
It was the World Cup after all.

Still, it was a great story that the wives and girlfriends
of the England team were this wild, crazy bunch. 'Hooli-
gans with credit cards' as one Spanish newspaper called us.

I had Claire with me for the whole tournament, and
various members of my family came out at different times,
so for a lot of it, I was busy with them. In fact, one of
the nice things about that trip was getting to know some
of the other players' families, who'd flown out to support
them. We morphed into one big group, the first and one

of the few times I've experienced that at an international tournament.

For a big occasion like the World Cup, a girl has to look her best, so before flying out for the tournament, I'd had new hair extensions put in. Now, I'm not generally high maintenance, day to day. I like to get my nails done, but I'm in my gym kit with my hair scraped back most days. I'm not the best at doing my hair and make-up at the best of times; I can just about manage the basics where make-up is concerned. I want to make more effort sometimes, but it's just down to time with me. I've always been the same.

These days, it makes me laugh when mums at the school say, 'Oh, you look nice,' when I've literally just washed and dried my hair and nothing else.

Now, I'd had extensions plenty of times before, but these were a bit of a faff because my usual hairdresser couldn't do them and I'd had to find an alternative. Not being great with make-up, my thinking was, at least my hair will look halfway decent while I'm there. Suffice to say, it didn't go well. Almost as soon as I arrived in Germany, the hair pieces, sewn-in wefts of hair, started to fall out.

Desperate to fix things, I called everywhere, trying to find a hairdresser who could work with that kind of extension – but no luck. With no one able to do it, all these terrible thoughts started going through my mind. With the world watching, I was about to go from having this lush long hair to a short straggly mop within a day. By then, they were literally hanging out of my head, and I was beside myself.

In the end, I got a flight home to get my bloody hair done – leaving my mum, Claire and my brother in Germany. I know it sounds diva-ish and dramatic, but I got in such a flap about it; flying back to get it sorted seemed like the only way. And we're not talking private jet or anything extravagant like that; it was Ryanair all the way.

When I got off the plane, I dashed straight home, where Wayne's cousin Leanne, who did extensions, met me. I sat down, she sewed my extensions back in, and I flew back to Germany on the next available flight. Panic over.

I never told anyone at the time – people must have wondered where the hell I'd disappeared to – but now you know.

England went out of the World Cup 3–1 on penalties after their quarter-final with Portugal ended in a 0–0 draw. It wasn't an easy match in any way. England lost David Beckham to injury just after half-time, and worse still, Wayne was sent off after a tangle with Ricardo Carvalho.

Carvalho had pulled him back, and then Wayne trod on his groin as Carvalho was on the floor. Carvalho's reaction was dramatic enough, but then his teammate Cristiano Ronaldo ran over to the referee demanding Wayne get a red card. When Wayne shoved Ronaldo away, that was it. He was off.

I watched the whole thing in horror, my eyes filling with tears. Suddenly my phone started pinging with messages. Live television pictures appeared to show Ronaldo winking towards the Portugal bench as Wayne made his way off the pitch. There was uproar amongst the England fans and supporters, and once it was all over, stories started appearing, inferring that their defeat was the fault of the players' wives and girlfriends. Right from the off, the press had decided on their narrative regarding the so-called WAGs. We were there to be criticised and ridiculed. In truth, we shopped, and we went out and enjoyed ourselves. A journalist called Oliver Holt wrote: 'The WAGs did very little apart from enjoy themselves in the way well-off young women would.' And he was right. The suggestion that we were a distraction to the players and in some way responsible for England being knocked out of the tournament was ridiculous. After the tournament, Wayne and I took a holiday; on a yacht around the French Riviera with six of our friends. We flew to France by private jet, then took a helicopter into Monaco before sailing to St Tropez and on to Cannes. It all felt very glamorous, and the yacht was beautiful, with four bedrooms and en-suite bathrooms; then there was a dining room, living room, kitchen and bedrooms where the crew slept. It was a wonderful break after the stresses of the World Cup, but I could see how upset Wayne was about losing and what had happened in that final match. 'Try to let it go,'

I told him. 'There'll be more chances, more World Cups to look forward to.'

'Yeah, I'll try,' he said with a smile.

We were drifting in the sea off this stunning French coastline, and for a while, all seemed right with the world.

Chapter Eight

Paul Stretford is the football agent who's looked after and represented Wayne for years. When I started dating Wayne he was with another agent, but signed with Paul soon afterwards. Once I started getting some attention in the press, the only contact they had was Paul, so his agency, Proactive Sports Management, naturally took care of that side of things for me. When requests and offers of work started coming in, Paul took on my representation fully. I needed somebody to answer press enquiries and negotiate offers that came through, and as Paul's team were dealing with Wayne's career, it seemed logical for them to look after me too. True, he was a football agent rather than a talent agent, but he knew his way around a contract and how to negotiate a good deal, and right then that was all I needed.

Within the organisation, there's always been someone on the team who works closely with me. For a long time, I had Jane Aspinall, who's still a good friend, and we've had some great times over the years. Now I have Stephanie

Lamon, who's worked with Paul for fifteen years. She started as a PA, but now I'm starting to get back into work post-kids, she's stepping in to manage stuff for me. It's nice for me to have a woman overseeing things like TV appearances and photo shoots, and Steph is highly organised and on the ball. Paul still focuses on the contractual and business side of things, and while I enjoy his company, he's not particularly interested in fashion or glamour. I don't have a PR team, but we'll bring somebody in whenever the need arises. I suppose I could have, at some point, gone to a more entertainment-based agent, but over the years, the deals Paul has done for both Wayne and me have been fantastic, so what would be the point?

One of my first projects was a column in *Closer* magazine that started in July 2006 and ran for two years. I liked the fresh, young approach of the magazine at that time, and I was excited to be asked to write for it. I did a media studies course at school, and for work experience, I had spent time working on a magazine that went out to various schools, interviewing, writing and researching.

The *Closer* column was a diary of what I was up to, where I'd been going, the music I was into, and bits and pieces about fashion and beauty. It was all quite innocent and fun, but it took me a while to get my head around the idea that people might be interested in what I had to say or what moisturiser I used to keep my skin looking fresh. Back then, there was no Instagram or TikTok, and who'd ever heard the term 'influencer' in 2004? In some ways, I suppose I was just doing what an influencer does now on their Instagram stories – just in print rather than online.

Still, it was a great thing for me to do. It wasn't exactly journalism, but it was me. This was something I might have pursued had I carried on with school and gone to university. A features writer for magazines – I could see myself doing that.

As well as that, there was the offer to be the face of George at ASDA, the clothing range. That was a big deal; I was suddenly earning good money doing something I enjoyed. Not that I'd ever thought of myself as model material. As far as I was concerned, I was a public figure wearing their clothes, and it was just great fun.

My friends were made up with my George at ASDA deal because I sometimes got them freebies – and let's face it, most girls love a freebie when it comes to fashion. There was one particular dress I got for them and they all went mad for at the time – black with a pretty grey and white pattern. The problem was, with us all hanging out together the whole time, there was one particular Friday night when we all turned up wearing that same dress. It was a bit embarrassing, but at least no one could accuse me of not flying the flag for the brand I was representing. After that, we planned and coordinated ahead of time, making sure none of us wore the same outfit as anyone else.

For me, these contracts and partnerships meant

independence and the opportunity to contribute finan-cially to the household and our joint account. I was proud of myself, and I suppose I felt justification for my decision to leave school when I did. The best thing about these jobs was they weren't nine-to-five gigs, so I could still travel with Wayne when the opportunity arose.

I knew how fortunate I was, even back then. I was living a life many young people only dreamed about. I never took it for granted and always tried to keep my feet firmly planted. Honestly, with a family like mine, I wouldn't have gotten away with anything else.

Vogue was one of the biggest surprises in those early days – back in 2005. I'd known of the iconic fashion magazine forever because my auntie Tracy often bought it, and I loved flicking through the glossy pages, devouring all the glamour.

I was in London, having lunch at The Wolseley with Wayne, when it all started. I think it might have been Val-entine's Day, and we were going to see 'We Will Rock You' at The Dominion Theatre later that evening.

I remember a woman coming over to chat with us at our table. I don't remember her name after all these years, but it turned out that she was connected with *Vogue*, and after our chat, she went back to them and suggested I would be someone worth featuring in the magazine.

I wasn't sure how I felt when I was first asked about it.

I was nervous, to be honest. Until then, in the press, I'd often been portrayed as some shopaholic chav, certainly not the kind of person who'd be gracing the pages of the world's number one fashion bible. As much as I love the idea of a glamorous *Vogue* photo shoot, there was the interview that went along with it to consider. What would they want to ask me? How in-depth would it be? Was I prepared to answer any tricky questions that might get thrown at me – especially regarding my relationship with Wayne? Until then, I still hadn't spoken publicly about the brothel scandal, and I wasn't sure I wanted to.

Being in the public eye at such a young age meant being prepared. OK, so it's probably the case, whatever your age and status, but I think you have to be extra vigilant when you're younger. That's when the public and the media are still forming their opinions about you, and if you're not used to those curveball questions in interviews and you say the wrong thing, you're in trouble. I'm a girl who can blabber on a mile a minute on all sorts of topics, but if one or two phrases get pulled out of context and go down on the page, there's nothing I can do about it. Once it's out there, in black and white, you don't always get to explain precisely what you meant or what you were trying to say. So, as lovely as being splashed across the pages of the world's foremost fashion magazine sounded, the last thing I wanted was a beautiful photo shoot coupled with some car crash of an interview to accompany it.

With everything that had happened over that year, I decided to turn it down. It was deeply disappointing but safer.

They were amazed at my decision. The magazine's artistic director, Alexandra Shulman, called and asked the question, 'Where will you get better pictures taken?'

She had a point. After Paul spoke to the people at *Vogue*, making sure they knew what kind of questions I would and wouldn't be comfortable with, I agreed to the piece.

Over the years, my approach to stuff like that hasn't changed much. In writing this book and with the new documentary I'm working on with Disney+, I have time to express myself in the way I want to. I've got time to get to know the people I'm collaborating with on the projects, and I can have my say on what goes in and what doesn't. In those situations, I'm far more comfortable being frank than I am in a magazine interview or a brief slot on a chat show. I'm happy tackling more complex subjects if I have time to say my piece. It's something I've learned the hard way and now have an instinct for. It doesn't matter how big or attractive an offer to do something seems; if I don't feel comfortable about it, I won't do it.

I was even the same with the recent libel case. To make that go away without going through the hell of it, I'd have to say something I didn't want to say and knew to be untrue – that I'd made a mistake. Sure, it would have been a quick fix, but then I'd have to live with it, regretting it every time a story about the case came up.

The *Vogue* shoot took place in an old house in Clapham, and I travelled down to London with my mum and aunt Tracy. I was nervous, of course. This was *Vogue*, and there I was, the girl who loved Top Shop and H&M, being photographed by Robert Wyatt, wearing clothes by the likes of Stella McCartney, Gucci and YSL. I was surrounded by stylists, make-up artists and hairdressers who were used to working with the *crème de la crème* of the fashion world, supermodels and film stars. It felt like a dream, or like someone was having a joke at my expense. Not that I'm putting myself down or being overly modest, but at that time, it was hard to get my head around the idea that I – Coleen McLoughlin – would be gracing those illustrious glossy pages. No puffa jacket or canary yellow moon boots required.

I needn't have worried. Everyone on the shoot was lovely, and Justine Picardie, who did the interview while I was getting ready, was fantastic. By the end of the shoot, my nerves had turned to excitement. I'd had a wonderful day and felt very special.

A lot came my way after the 2006 World Cup – offers of endorsements and a chance to help create new things in my name as a brand. One was the opportunity to create my own fragrance, an idea I loved and jumped at. I went over to France to work with the perfumers, where I learned how everything was done and chose the ingredients for what was to become my signature scent. As excited as I was, I wouldn't have been interested in putting my name on something that I hadn't been involved in creating. I wanted to have input.

There was a Chanel perfume called Chance Eau Fraîche that I loved at the time, citrus and pink pepper top notes and heart notes of iris and jasmine. That was the inspiration for my fragrance, which we built and blended from the bottom up. My first perfume was simply called Coleen, and later we made Butterfly, which was even more exciting because we launched it in Selfridges. Of course, my mum, aunties, cousins, and all my girlfriends came to that one.

A year or so after the fragrance launched, I worked with designers on a jewellery and watch range for Argos. That came around the time of my first TV show, *Coleen's Real Women*.

I loved the idea of the show straight off – that ordinary women of all shapes, sizes and heights could do the jobs and participate in advertising campaigns usually reserved for skinny, six-foot models. In 2008, when the show was made, there was nothing like it out there, so the concept appealed to me. After all, there were plenty of women with great or unusual faces who'd doubtless be overlooked for campaigns just because they weren't the right body shape or height. This felt like something important.

The only problem was that I hadn't done much TV,

and the bits and pieces I had done weren't proper hosting gigs like this one. I was nervous – I mean, the show had my name in the title, for goodness' sake!

My saving grace was that *Real Women* was a brand-new show for everyone, from the director to the crew and beyond. It had never been done before, so we were all learning on the job. We all took the same gamble, not knowing if the public would take to it or even watch.

Camilla Johnson-Hill was a fashion director working with lots of big brands in the fashion industry, and she was to be my co-host on the project. She really knew her stuff as far as the subject of models and modelling campaigns was concerned, but like me, she was also relatively new when it came to doing telly, so we could help and support one another as the show progressed. She was a fantastic on-screen partner, and we've remained friends since the show ended.

It was hard work, however. I'd do Monday to Friday in London, using the Charlotte Street Hotel as my base, then I'd travel home for the weekends. I had no kids then, if you don't count Wayne, which made it much more manageable. I'm not sure I could have done it having had the boys – there were times when the process exhausted me, and I'd crumble.

As it happened, the show turned out wonderfully, and the feedback I got was inspiring. Everywhere I went, women and young girls would come up to me, either telling me how much they appreciated and loved the idea of giving ordinary women a chance to do extraordinary things or asking how they might get involved.

'It's about time,' people would say, and I agreed wholeheartedly.

By the time we went into a second series, I felt a lot more confident – everyone did. By then, we knew what worked and what didn't, and we didn't spend loads of time devising and shooting a ton of content that ultimately wouldn't make it into the show.

Still, the days were long and tiring. Sometimes, I felt overwhelmed by the amount we had to get done. It was regular for a final filming slot to be set but then changed and for filming to drag on several days longer than promised.

On the final day of shooting the series, on location in Glasgow with a fake-tan company, I was exhausted beyond belief. That afternoon, I was due to get the flight home in time for a girls' night out in Liverpool. It wasn't anything super-fancy, just a night in a local pub for one of my mates' birthdays. After so many weeks away, not seeing my friends, I had my heart set on going, but there was a hitch. As the day wore on, we found out that filming was going to run over, and there was no way I'd be able to catch the flight in time to get home. In fact, I'd have to catch a flight the following morning.

Now, I'm not a diva – I promise. That day, though, I was stressed and emotional – desperate to finally get home after so long away – so the news did not go down at all well.

I got on the phone with Paul, fuming. 'This is not on, Paul! They told me I'd be able to go on time. There's been so many times I've been told this was my final day, but it's gone on longer, and I've gone along with it. This time, I'm not having it.' I really threw my toys out of the pram.

Paul said, 'I'll sort it.'

A short while later, he called me back. 'There's a private jet waiting for you at Glasgow Airport,' he said.

I have to say, as relieved and happy as I was, I did feel slightly embarrassed. I wasn't flying to Monte Carlo or some swanky unmissable awards ceremony; I was off to The Lobster in Croxteth – on a private jet. Still, I'd promised my mate I'd be at her birthday drinks, so I was going. When we finally wrapped up for the day, I took a car to Glasgow Airport, then I got on that private jet back to Liverpool and went straight to the pub to join my mates.

OK, so it was a bit of a diva strop, but as I've said, I'm very organised; I'm one for details so I can plan accordingly. The lesson here is, don't promise me something's happening if it isn't. I can't work with that.

These were all big moments, and much as I loved having these fantastic opportunities, I sometimes questioned why my name was enough to sell a brand or product people might want to buy and wear or a TV show they might watch. I still question it to this day. After all these years I, of course, understand how celebrity branding and endorsements can be a powerful thing. Still, it's not something I've ever taken for granted.

I recently did a campaign for my friend Justine's store, Cricket, in Liverpool, where I've shopped for years. She was launching a new website and wanted people from Liverpool who embodied the store's brand to feature in the photo shoot, so she asked my eldest son Kai and me. After the launch, Justine asked if I'd co-host a dinner with her in London along with filmmaker Alec Maxwell, the husband of *Vogue* editor Edward Enninful, who was the campaign's creative director. I was flattered to be asked, but I wasn't sure she'd made the right choice of co-host.

'If you put my name on the invitation, do you really think people will want to come?' I asked her in a voice note.

She messaged back – '*OMG are you crazy? Can't believe you would think like that. You'd only enhance, and you're from the community.*'

It's funny that I still harbour those doubts about myself after all this time. Maybe it's because up until recently – before the story leaks and subsequent court case – I'd been out of the limelight for quite a few years, just being a mum and thoroughly enjoying it. I'd love to have as much confidence in myself with the wider world as I do within my friends, family and social group, but I often don't.

A few days later, someone sent me a message suggesting

I relaunch the perfume range as it was her favourite fragrance. I guess that was a sign.

Being a mum of four has meant me stepping back from work, but now all my children are at school, I've got a hankering to get back into it. It would have to fit in with the kids' timetables, of course, but if the right project comes along, I'm ready for it.

Chapter Nine

I love a party, always have. Not always just regular parties either, I really enjoy a theme. Over the years, I've had
a silent disco, a zoo-themed party with glow sticks and
animal-print face-painting, and roller-disco for the kids,
amongst many others.

My *Sex and the City* girls-only party in 2010 was quite mad.
My idea for this shindig was based on the *Sex and the City 2*
movie, where the women fly out to Abu Dhabi for an all-
expenses-paid trip, with Samantha devising a PR campaign
for an Arab sheikh's business venture. When my girlfriends,
my mum and mum's cousin turned up at my place, they were
surprised and slightly confused to find a camel in the garden,
which I'd rented for the occasion. Yes, I rented a camel. It's
very much about the detail when I'm throwing a party. I
also love buying and wrapping gifts, and at one time, I'd buy
Christmas presents for virtually everyone I knew and their
families and kids. For a number of years, you could find me
driving around Liverpool in a borrowed van a few days before
Christmas, delivering them all, like a Scouse Mrs Claus.

Most of all, I get a kick out of bringing people together, and as much as I can I've always included my mum, dad, brothers and close friends in everything I do. Even as a kid, my parents knew everyone I was mixing with – all my friends – and it's no different now. At concerts or going to the races, Mum will bring her friends along, and they'll come together with all my mates in one big social circle. That's always been my way; it makes me happy to help that happen.

It was very much what I wanted for our wedding in 2008. We'd decided on a smaller wedding after the experience I'd had with my twenty-first birthday party, which was held at Thornton Manor Country Estate in Birkenhead. For that, I had a marquee in the grounds, fairground rides and a performance by Sugababes, so not exactly understated as parties go. Still, while it had been a fabulous all-singing, all-dancing event, and I'd had a great night, I'd also felt overwhelmed. There were so many people there; I spent much of the night chatting to my guests and being the hostess. I didn't have time to take a breath and appreciate it, and then it was over before I knew it. I didn't want our wedding to be like that. I wanted something intimate with the people that knew us best and were closest to us. Of course, it could be beautiful and glamorous, but I wanted a relaxed wedding, with several events over four days rather than one big blowout.

Inviting around sixty people to join us in Italy was a

hard decision. I love all my family and friends, but I knew I couldn't have everyone. Inevitably, a few people were left disappointed, but that was the tough decision we'd made.

We organised the wedding with events planner Julie Perry, who worked with a company called Revellers – a company we'd worked with several times before on various parties. Once we'd announced the wedding, there were magazine offers to cover it, and we decided to go with *OK!* magazine.

When a publication like that is on board, they organise a lot of security around the event to ensure nothing gets out before the piece comes out in the magazine, which was also great for us. Initially, I was a bit concerned about how invasive it might be to have photographers and journalists darting around at our wedding, but the team they sent wasn't at all intrusive. They managed to get what they needed while staying pretty much in the background, and they all joined in with the celebrations when they were able. And, of course, the photos were beautiful.

I threw myself into the planning and enjoyed the process; it was exciting watching it all come together. Wayne wasn't interested in all the ins and outs of venues, parties and wedding attire. Not because he wasn't bothered; he's just very laid back and trusts me to pull something out of the bag without him having to worry.

'Just do whatever you want to do,' was his line, which was good enough for me.

I didn't need telling twice. He's the same when it comes to what goes in our house. He'll have a few specifications of things he'd like but leaves most of it to me.

'Even if I did make a suggestion, she'd end up getting her own way if she didn't like it,' he sometimes says with a smile.

And yeah, he's pretty much on the money with that one.

You won't be surprised to hear that I had a fair few dresses to carry me across the four days of celebrations – practically a full collection. I had one for our first night party, another for the pre-wedding meal, one for the registry office, the wedding dress, and two for the reception because I couldn't decide what I wanted – long and elegant or a short party number. Ultimately, it came down to how I felt on the day, and I went for the party dress. Oh yes, and then there was another dress for the barbeque we threw the day after the wedding.

When choosing the wedding dress, we made a girls' trip to London. Mum, me, my nan and my auntie Tracy, plus my friend Justine, from Cricket. She'd offered to advise and guide me regarding the dress. We went to Brown's Brides, Harrods, Alice Temperley and Amanda Wakeley Bridal – I really did the rounds. With the wedding being in Italy, I was thinking something simple and straight – evening gown style rather than big and traditional.

I didn't see anything that day, but through various

people we met, I was introduced to the women behind the Marchesa label, Keren Craig and Georgina Chapman, who were based in New York. I already had some of their dresses and loved them, so I decided they were the right people to design my wedding dress – plus the bridesmaids' dresses and all my other dresses – the whole collection.

In time, they came up with some ideas and sent me some sketches before my mum and I flew to New York to meet them at their studio. Being so into fashion, that whole design process fascinated me – I loved being part of it and seeing it all come together. After trying various wedding dress ideas, the one that I thought I wouldn't go for was the one I absolutely loved. A plain bodice with a big, detailed, organza skirt.

My hen do was a trip to Miami – me and five friends. We all flew out business class, which was a real treat, so after a few drinks on the flight, we were all giddy and excited about the days to follow. By the time we got off the flight, we were a bit more than just giddy, and one of my friends set some alarm off at the airport, which we all found hilarious.

One of my mates wasn't able to get the time off work, so, not wanting to miss out on the trip of a lifetime, she took it off sick – signed off with a bad back. Now, being in Miami with me, we all knew there was every chance she was going to be photographed, with the possibility of her picture landing up in the papers and her bosses seeing it.

Was she worried? No! Her answer was to wear a massive pair of sunglasses everywhere she went. It was like they were glued to her face. That way, if she did get papped and ended up in the *Daily Mail* or *Heat* magazine, no one would recognise her. Still, there was a ridiculous amount of press interest around my wedding and hen do.

On one night out, there were shots of me angled to make it look as though I was chatting up some lad, which, of course, was not the case. This was a girl's-only party, none of us had the slightest interest in flirting with random men – especially the bride-to-be. There were also shots of us enjoying ourselves in the hotel pool, and that's when my friend ended up in the paper, as clear as day.

She returned to work the following week with massive white circles around her eyes where she'd been in the sun so long but refused to remove the glasses. Everyone at her work was taking the piss.

'Oh, we saw you in the paper in that pool. That water therapy must have done wonders for your sore back!'

I had another hen party when we got home – a spa day at The Lowry Hotel in Manchester and a night out at a club called Panacea. My nan came that night, bless her, but while we were all knocking back the drinks, she was on pots of tea, which looked quite mad in the middle of a swanky nightclub. She didn't care – she was happy!

The wedding was in Santa Margherita, a fishing village on the Italian Riviera near Genoa. Wayne and I flew out a few days before everyone arrived to register and finalise some other bits and pieces. We'd booked the same boutique hotel for everyone, and all our guests came on the same flight; it was quite the invasion.

On the first night, we had a party on a yacht just off the coast. Well, when I say a party, it was actually a bit more than that – we threw a masquerade ball. All our guests were dressed up to the nines, and as the boat wasn't returning to the dock until 2 a.m., there was no getting off once you were aboard.

Of course, the girls all went to town with fabulous evening gowns. The only problem was that they'd factored heels into their outfits, and when you're on a boat, you have to take your shoes off, which I hadn't thought of. Consequently, all the women were wandering around with their beautiful dresses trailing along the deck while a pile of exquisite party shoes sat redundantly in the corner.

It was such a special night. I have a lovely memory of standing at the front of the boat with a few of my friends from Croxteth as it pulled away from the harbour.

'Look how beautiful this is.' It felt surreal to be on that amazing yacht looking over the water and the Italian coastline with these girls I'd grown up with; the girls I'd hung out with in the park or by the parade of shops, night after night.

'We haven't done bad for a gang of girls from Crocky, have we?' my friend Christina said. 'Take it all in, girls!'

I remember thinking I would never take these moments for granted and always be grateful. 'Yeah, let's take it all in and never forget it.'

Later in the evening, my dad, who loves to entertain a crowd, jumped into the jacuzzi, fully clothed in his tuxedo, drenching everyone in a close radius. As I said before, my family will always be the ones to bring me back down to earth.

After a few hours, when my nan and grandad got tired, I suggested they have a lie down in one of the bedrooms.

'OK, just make sure you wake us up when yous all get off,' Nan said to Sophia, one of my younger cousins.

Wayne and I were the only ones sleeping on the boat; we'd planned a romantic lunch the following day, facing the spot where we were due to have our wedding ceremony while everyone else was back at the hotel.

The following morning, I was coming down a spiral staircase on the boat, feeling relaxed and happy, when I spotted a flash of fabric through the stair rungs. *Hang on,* I thought, *that looks like the dress my nan had on last night.* Sure enough, when I got to the bottom of the stairs, there she was, my nan, still fully clothed in the previous night's outfit.

'Oh my word, Coleen,' she said, panic-stricken. 'We're shipwrecked; we're lost at sea. Our Sophia never woke us up, and when I've opened my eyes and looked out the window, we're floating in the middle of the ocean. What are we going to do?'

'It's fine, Nan,' I said. 'We're not shipwrecked, we're just having a day out on the boat, and you and grandad can join us.'

'Oh no, love, we can't ruin your day,' she said.

'It's fine, Nan, we're only having lunch; yous can spend the day with Wayne and me.'

So, my nan ended up wearing a spare pair of my knickers and a maxi dress while Grandad put on one of Wayne's polo tops, and they were all set. The funny thing was, because my grandad smoked, he just sat on the deck with a ciggie most of the day and, not thinking, didn't have a scrap of sun cream on him. Also, he hadn't worn short sleeves for years; he only ever wore long sleeves, so his arms hadn't seen the sun in ages.

After enjoying a beautiful lunch on board, the boat drifted back to the dock, and we all returned to the hotel. But when my grandad came down for dinner that night, he was burnt to a crisp.

That was the evening we had the big pre-wedding dinner at the hotel, and afterwards, I went with Mum and my bridesmaids to stay on the yacht while everyone else carried on with the festivities. I didn't find out until the next day, but things got lively after we'd left. Very lively, in fact. The story went that the hotel staff had told some of the more enthusiastic guests to turn the music off and go to bed. When that didn't happen, the police were called to settle things down. There was no trouble and, thank goodness, no one ended up in a cell, but the hotel was in a residential area, and people were starting to complain.

Wayne and I were due at the registry office the following morning with our parents, Wayne's best man, my uncle Shaun, and my maid of honour, Claire. This was just the more official side of things – the legal bit – and we decided to get it done in the morning before the ceremony.

'Make sure you get a shave,' was the only instruction I'd given Wayne.

It wasn't the main event, but I wanted us to look halfway decent while signing the register.

I arrived first with Mum and Claire, and when Wayne and Shaun turned up with his parents and my dad, they were all wearing sunglasses. It wasn't sunny. No, they were all red-eyed and hung-over. To top it all, no razor had been anywhere near Wayne's face – he'd turned up with sprouts of uneven stubble all over the place. I later discovered if it hadn't been for his mum literally dragging him out of bed, he wouldn't have even made it there.

Seeing this motley crew shuffling towards us, I turned to Claire.

'Thank goodness the wedding's not till five,' I said.

That part of the proceedings was short and sweet, but I ended up shedding a tear. It dawned on me that although I'd been with Wayne for years, this was another step into the unknown, becoming a wife. I'd no longer be Coleen McLoughlin; my family name would be gone, and I'd be taking someone else's name. Silly I know, but there was a pang of sadness inside me.

The venue for the main event was an old monastery with a lovely chapel and grounds and a gorgeous space for the reception. I got ready at the venue, and it was all very relaxed because I'd given myself plenty of time for hair, make-up and all the rest. Still, when my dad walked into the room, all ready to walk me down the aisle, I burst into tears. I was just so overwhelmed by the day and the idea that I would spend the rest of my life as somebody's wife. My mum and dad had been blessed with a solid and loving marriage. Could I live up to that? Even though Wayne and I had been dating for years and already lived together, this felt different. It was such a massive commitment. Could we have the kind of marriage my parents had enjoyed for so long?

When I looked up at my dad, he was teary-eyed as well, which made me even worse. I ended up back in the make-up chair, getting my face touched up again because now I had mascara running down my cheeks. So, after all that time I'd given myself to get ready, I was late walking down the aisle. Apparently, there were a few whispers of 'Where is she?' among the congregation before I appeared. I wonder if a few people thought I'd done a runner. As I entered the church, a poem I had recorded for my dad was played. The sentiment behind it was that even though I'd found a man to love and spend the rest of my life with, I would always be a daddy's girl.

My bridesmaids were my cousins Carly and Sophia, my sister Rosie and Wayne's cousin's little girl Grace, and Wayne had my brothers and his as ushers. Our parish priest, Father Ned from St Teresa's, had flown out to marry us, which meant a lot to me. He went on to christen Kai, Klay and Kit and remains a close family friend. The ceremony he performed was every bit as beautiful as I'd hoped it would be. I was overcome with happiness.

We had Westlife sing at our reception and for our first dance – a complete surprise to all the guests – while the best man's speech was a surprise to Wayne and me.

For that, my cousin and one of Wayne's mates had made a corresponding slideshow depicting key moments from our past, with them playing us. In costume, they'd re-enacted Wayne's proposal at the petrol garage, a night when I came home from a club to find Wayne climbing through my bedroom window at our old house, worried because he couldn't reach me, and another of Wayne in the terrible red leather jacket he'd bought – one of many poor fashion choices he made in those early days.

Still, as with every party I've ever organised, this one ran on later than it was supposed to. Everyone was having such a great time, though, so I told the DJ to keep playing and he was more than happy to. At one point it started raining, a light drizzle at first, then it came lashing down.

'I'll have to finish soon, Coleen, the sound system is getting soaked!' the DJ said.

He played Rihanna's 'Umbrella', and we all danced in the pouring rain, arms in the air, getting drenched. By the time the song ended, it was an utter deluge, so everyone scattered, running in all directions to the transport which was waiting to take them back to the hotel. Wayne and I were staying in a room at the venue, so we didn't have far to go.

For the barbeque the next day, I'd booked Kelly Jones and Adam Zindani from Stereophonics to do an acoustic set. That was my wedding present to Wayne – they're his all-time favourite band, and he was made up.

Our honeymoon was in Las Vegas; we'd booked a week staying at the Wynn and planned on flying to Hawaii for our second week. With the football season at an end, a few of our friends happened to be in Vegas at the same time. We had so much fun that, in the end, we cancelled Hawaii and stayed in Vegas for the whole two weeks.

Apart from having the children, I can honestly say, our Italian wedding excursion was the best four days of my life. Of the sixty who came to celebrate with us, some had never met, but by the end of it, new friendships had been made on both sides. People were swapping phone numbers and planning to meet up back in the UK. In fact, despite all the glitz and glamour of the occasion, that was the best thing about it – the people who came, the perfect mix of loved ones, all getting on so brilliantly. I genuinely believe we could have had the wedding in a caravan in Wales, and that group of friends and close family would still have made it special.

Chapter Ten

We were both over the moon when I discovered I was pregnant in late 2008. That was until I started bleeding one morning at about ten weeks. After an examination at the hospital, doctors told us there was a heartbeat but that the baby was smaller than it should have been at ten weeks. Despite that, they seemed confident that all was well, and I went home feeling relieved.

Later that same night, I started to bleed again, this time much heavier. We rushed back to the hospital, where the doctors told me I was miscarrying. Of course, we were both devastated by the news. Still, as it was happening at the hospital, no further procedure was necessary. I went home feeling shaken up and hollow. It's a strange thing to be feeling all that excitement and joy, only to have it taken away so fast – a horrible experience which knocked Wayne for six too.

Back at home that night, he cried. He'd been desperate to be a dad, and I could see on his face how wrecked he was with the loss.

'It's awful,' he said. 'I know you've been through such a terrible experience, but it's hard for me as well.'

I think he just had to voice his feelings, which wasn't something he did all that often. It stayed with him for quite a while afterwards, probably right up until I got pregnant again.

It was strange for the next few weeks; I didn't really know how to feel about what had happened. I was concerned for sure. This had been my first pregnancy, and things had gone wrong. I couldn't help wondering what this meant – was I going to be one of those unlucky women who couldn't carry a baby, who couldn't have kids? I thought about my mum. Although she never miscarried, she'd really struggled with getting pregnant – it took her years, and she went through a lot of fertility treatment. Mum suggested that the fact I'd actually got pregnant meant that this probably wasn't going to be the case for me and that I just had to try again. That gave me hope.

More women have miscarriages than I'd imagined. Once I told a few close friends and family about my experience, people told me how it had happened to them, their friends, or someone they worked with. It was so much more common than I'd imagined. This is the first time I've spoken about it outside that close circle because, at the time, we just wanted to deal with it in our own way, without outside attention – which is why I was relieved the press never found out about it.

Thankfully, I did get pregnant again not long after, and that wonderful news lifted us back up again. This time I wasn't taking any chances. I was careful, looked after myself, and had more check-ups and scans than I probably needed – just to keep my mind at rest. Because of what had happened the first time around, I couldn't enjoy the first part of the pregnancy. I was always slightly on edge, wondering if I might lose this baby too.

Unfortunately for us, the press got wind of my pregnancy news slightly earlier than we would have liked, just before I reached that all-important twelve-week mark. Paul phoned one morning to say that a paper had somehow got hold of the story – although he had no clue how. Until then, I'd told virtually no one, like most people, pre-twelve-week scan. Once I knew it was about to be made public, I told the family and close friends who didn't already know. I didn't want the first time they heard about it to be in a newspaper, and there was certainly no way we were going to be able to stop the story, so that felt like the best way forward.

Now I could get excited about the prospect of being a mum, and once I was over the twelve-week hurdle, I started to relax a bit more. The prospect of having another human being to look after – besides Wayne – made me feel like I was finally blossoming into a mature woman. The whole family were over the moon. Ours was to be the first grandchild on both sides and the first nephew for any of our siblings, so this was truly something beautiful.

Now, after four kids, I don't really remember too much about that first pregnancy other than it feeling like something new was happening to my body – that and all the weight I put on. Throughout that pregnancy, I relaxed, ate what I wanted, and didn't really exercise. Getting back into shape after Kai was tough, so with the other three, I kept up the exercise and didn't overindulge.

One thing that has stayed consistent through my pregnancies is that I've never experienced going into labour naturally, despite giving birth four times. My first three, Kai, Klay and Kit, were lazy boys who didn't want to come out, so I always had to be induced.

I tried everything with Kai before that happened – all the tips and old wives' tales. I drank raspberry leaf tea, bounced up and down on an exercise ball, ate pineapple and hot curries. I was so desperate, I even drank castor oil, which I really don't recommend unless you want to spend several revolting hours on the toilet.

For my fourth child, Cass, we planned the time. With the first three being late, I figured the fourth wouldn't be any different. Wayne was playing for Everton then and was flying to Dubai for a training camp. Not wanting him to miss the birth, I went in to be induced a few days before he was due to leave, as I was already full-term.

Before I went in to have Kai, I did all the essential stuff a first-time mum might do, meaning I went for a Chinese with my family, had a spray tan and then got my hair blow-dried. There was no reason to do all this other than to make myself feel good, and why not? I had plenty of time on my hands after all.

There'd been so much talk in the press about where and when I was having the baby; I wanted to be prepared for all eventualities. We'd taken out an injunction so nobody could publish a picture of the baby's face, but there were still photographers camped outside the hospital when we arrived.

My dad dropped me off on a Sunday night at about 9.30 p.m., leaving my mum, Wayne and me at the hospital. As we got to the entrance, there was a group of women outside getting some fresh air – proper Scousers – smiling and waving at us.

'Oh, Coleen, good luck, love!'

It wasn't at all how I'd imagined it would be. I thought I'd be rushed in with contractions and labour pains rather than strolling through the door with my mum trotting along behind, carrying her and Wayne's snack essentials.

It was quite a while after I'd popped the pill to induce labour that things started to move, but suddenly it was all happening. When it came to the birth, I had it set in my mind that I wanted to feel something. Not that I wanted to be in screaming agony, but I at least wanted to have the sensation of pushing as the baby was being born. I was determined to be there in the moment as much as possible, so I decided against having diamorphine. That, or any kind of anaesthetic, always makes me sick, so as far as I was concerned, that was out of the question. I certainly didn't want my lingering memory to be one of nausea.

Suddenly, though, my blood pressure was sky-high, and we were told the baby was in distress.

'Coleen, if you don't have an epidural or some pain relief, we're going to have to take you down for an emergency C-section,' the midwife told me.

That was the last thing I wanted, so I agreed to an epidural, which brought my blood pressure down straight away. The positive was I could still feel the contractions in my stomach to an extent, so although I was no longer in great pain, I could feel when I should push. I've had epidurals every time since.

I wanted my dad in the room when Kai was born. I suppose some people might think that a bit odd, but for me, it was a moment I wanted us all to share. I wanted Dad to be able to say he was there when his first grandchild came into the world. Of course, he was fairly cautious about where he stood – he didn't go down the bottom end of the bed – but having him with me was lovely.

Wayne was nervous throughout and hated seeing me in pain. I remember the look on his face when the midwife announced, 'I can see the baby's hair.' He was clearly in two minds about whether he wanted to check it out for himself or just take the midwife's word for it. Once Kai was in the world, the midwife put my new baby on me, skin-to-skin, and then Wayne took his top off and held his new son.

My dad was the one who cut Kai's cord; Wayne was too nervous. Over the course of having our four children, that particular job has been passed around the family. Wayne – more confident the second time – cut Klay's cord, Mum cut Kit's, and when I had Cass, the job went to his older brother Kai, who was eight at the time and fascinated by the whole process of my pregnancy. The arrival of another baby brother was so exciting for him, so he'd asked if he could be there when Cass was born. I couldn't let him be there as I was giving birth, that would have been a bit much. But my dad brought him in right after so he could cut his new brother's cord.

Once Kai was finally out in the world, the family on both sides came to the hospital to celebrate. Mum had told my dad to bring some champagne up to the visitors' room, and at first, I'd thought that might be a nice idea. I pictured myself, sitting serenely on the bed, looking pristine with my new baby at my side and a glass of bubbly in my hand. In reality, things were very different. I could certainly hear corks popping and everyone having a good time in the next room, but the thought of sipping champagne was the furthest thing from my mind after giving birth. In fact, I couldn't think of anything worse.

Later, when Kai was settled in his tiny crib, the nurse

asked, 'Have you got the feeling in your legs back, Coleen? Can you walk back to your room?'

I wiggled my toes and felt the sensation, so I assumed the epidural had worn off.

'Yeah, all good,' I said, hauling myself up with the nurse's help.

The next thing I knew, I was on the floor. My toes might have been back in action, but the rest of my legs still had a way to go; it was like there was nothing there.

'You're going in a wheelchair,' the nurse said. 'Don't worry, we'll bring your things.'

I was wheeled along the corridor back to my room while nurses and hospital porters followed with vast amounts of luggage.

'Is this really all yours?' the nurse said.

As usual, I'd overpacked massively. Apart from the essentials, which I went above and beyond with, I'd brought a bag with candles and picture frames to help create the perfect ambience while giving birth – then there was the practical stuff: air freshener, Flash wipes. I'd brought it all.

After giving birth, I planned on staying with my mum for a week or so. Initially, this was just for a bit of support while I got used to things, what with Wayne being at work every day. Let's face it; if there was ever an expert on looking after young children, it was my mother. As much as I'd been looking forward to my baby's arrival, I wasn't the most confident of mums in those first weeks. In fact, a few days after I brought him home, it dawned on me what a life-changing event this was. Until then, Wayne and I had lived our lives just picking ourselves up and going wherever and whenever took our fancy. We had the luxury to do whatever we liked within reason and football permitting. I'd given up my studies and left school early to have that life, and now it was disappearing. It's funny; the changing nappies and sleepless nights side of things didn't faze me. It was more the realisation that I now had this little person for life. That's what made my head spin. OK, so Kai wasn't going to be a little person forever. But he was ours – mine and Wayne's – and we would be wholly responsible for him and everything that happened to him for a very long time.

Was I being selfish? Was I even up to the job? It's funny; I hadn't felt particularly worried or scared leading up to Kai's birth, but suddenly, all these thoughts bubbled up in my mind and took me over. Combined with exhaustion and hormones, it made for an explosive cocktail; I found myself in the grips of a proper meltdown.

Mum walked into her bedroom one morning to find me crying my heart out on her bed like the world was about to end.

'How do people do this?' I sobbed. 'How do these poor single mums cope with raising a baby alone?'

Mum looked confused. 'What are you talking about, love?'

I don't know why I'd suddenly fixated on the potential plight of single mums, but I had. I was tired and overwrought, so my mind was all over the place.

Mum sat down on the bed and spoke softly to me. 'I know what you're saying, love, but that's not you, is it? You're lucky enough to have Wayne and all of us to support you. You're fine, Coleen, you've got help, and you'll be a great mum.'

The fact that I'd got so upset made me feel silly for a while, full of guilt. Eventually, I pulled myself together and got real. I sat up on the bed, took a few deep breaths and thought about what my dad always said to us when we felt hard done by as kids or complained about missing out in some way.

'We're millionaires! We've got this house, we've got food, and we're healthy. We're millionaires.'

Dad was a firm believer in his millionaire mantra. If he ever went to get us a McDonald's as a treat from the drive-thru, he'd always take a plastic bag with him to pop the bag full of burgers, fries and milkshakes into. Back then, a McDonald's supper really was a treat. He didn't want any kids on our street whose families might not be able to afford one to see him bringing it home for us. Of course, we weren't millionaires financially or anything near, but he was right. In life, we were.

It was a similar story whenever we went to our holiday home in Barbados. Dad went to the church there. He'd catch the yellow Reggae bus and go with all the locals. One afternoon, he came back with no shoes on.

Mum looked down at his feet, confused. 'Where's your shoes gone?'

'Oh, I gave them to the homeless man who sits outside the church,' he said.

It got to be a regular thing. Every time we went to Barbados, Dad would take the man who sat outside the church a pair of shoes.

We haven't been there for a few years, but a couple we got friendly with over time have taken on the mantle when they go. One day, they phoned my mum out of the blue and asked, 'What size shoes does the man outside the church wear? We thought we'd take the shoes as you're not coming this year.'

I'm not sure they even attended the church; it was about keeping up my dad's tradition.

It's funny how those things have sat with me over the years. It's often how I calm myself down when I'm hit with a challenge or get in a state about something. I bring myself back down to earth by remembering how bloody fortunate I am and how many other people have it so much harder. Remembering all that helped me that day, as it always does.

In the end, that 'week or so' of staying at my mum's turned into a few months – primarily because I got so comfortable having the extra help. Probably a bit too comfortable. By the time I was finally back in my own home,

I felt more settled. Wayne was pretty good with feeds and nappy changing, and though it was all very new to him, he took to it reasonably well.

I still had shaky moments, though. At the end of the first football season after Kai was born, we took him to a family friend's house in Majorca. During our time there, Wayne was due to fly home to pick up an award.

'I'll fly home, collect the award and come straight back,' he promised.

He was being flown privately, so the plan was he'd only be away overnight, back the following morning. *That's OK,* I thought. *I can manage one night on my own.* The only thing was, I knew there'd be some kind of celebration after the awards ceremony. That fact sowed seeds of doubt in my mind, and of course, I was right to have worried.

That evening was warm and beautiful, so I went for a walk into town with the baby and then had an early night. The following morning, I called Wayne to find out how his night had gone. No answer. I left it a while and called again. No answer. His flight was a fairly early one, so shouldn't he have been in a car by now on his way to the airport?

I phoned Paul, who was staying at the same hotel as Wayne. 'Where is he? I can't get hold of him.'

'Let me see if he's in his room,' Paul said.

It turned out that he hadn't got up for his flight. It was a private charter, so it could be rescheduled, but the fact that he'd let it happen sent me into one.

'How could you? I'm halfway across the world, I've got a baby with me, and you've abandoned us here,' I told him when I finally got hold of him.

It was all very dramatic, but I was pissed off and still fragile. It was our first trip away with a new baby, and surely if I had to be a responsible parent now, then so did he.

'Look, I'm going to the airport now; I'll be back in a few hours,' Wayne said.

'You do that,' I said. 'Get on that plane.'

When he did finally arrive back, I couldn't bring myself to speak to him for the rest of that night. Normally, I'd have taken something like that in my stride, but I guess my hormones were still all over the place, so I probably had overdramatised.

Over time, travelling with the kids has been one of the joys of our lives, and we're lucky to have been on some incredible trips. Still, Wayne and I always try to get a week away on our own, and my mum and dad will move in and look after the kids. That's a little tradition we've always kept, and we're blessed to have that kind of family child-care at our disposal.

Mum was right, of course – as time went on, I was fine. Still, those doubts did cast a bit of a shadow in those first few weeks. I'm sure it's the same for many first-time mums. We think we can't cope; we think we don't know what to do. Generally, we always get there, don't we? We just need a bit of time.

Chapter Eleven

I always felt it was important to support Wayne when he was playing in an international tournament. I knew it was grounding and comforting for him to have his family around in those high-pressure situations, especially when he was away from home for some time with so much going on. It's the same now he's working in America as a manager. He can't come home during the football season, so whenever the kids are off and we have the chance, we'll fly over to be with him. It's sometimes a lot of organisation and effort, but I know it's vital that he sees us and that the children see him.

One of the few times I didn't attend a big tournament was the 2010 World Cup in South Africa. Besides Kai being a young baby, the matches were spread everywhere, so that would mean a lot of travelling. I thought it might be too much.

Instead, I stayed home, and we threw a big World Cup party at my mum's house for the first game. As usual, it turned into a big event with food, drinks, a marquee in the garden, and all of us wearing England themed outfits.

During the tournament, I got this weird pain in my head, around my eye. It didn't feel like a regular headache, and it was bloody persistent. I popped a couple of paracetamol and then a couple more, but it just wouldn't budge. Then, in the early hours of one morning, when England were due to play their next game, the pain got so bad that I asked my dad to take me to A&E.

By then, I was worried. My friend had recently got a message from a photographer who'd taken photos of me and noticed a strange glow in my eye when he looked back at some of the shots. He said there was a rare form of eye cancer that was sometimes picked up by camera flashes, showing up as a white glow, and suggested I get my eye checked. I hadn't taken much notice then, but suddenly I was thinking the worst. What if it was that? What if I had some sort of tumour behind my eye? By the time we reached the hospital, the pain had become unbearable, but the doctors in the A&E couldn't do much more than check me over and suggest I see an eye specialist as soon as possible.

Later that morning, through a contact at Man United, I found myself at Manchester Eye Hospital diagnosed with iritis, which is inflammation and swelling of the coloured ring around the iris. It turned out that I carry a gene that could cause reactive arthritis, which is a condition that causes painful swelling in various parts of the body, amongst other problems, and this was the first flare-up of something associated with it. An infection could bring it on, but stress was also something I had to watch, as that was often a contributing factor.

It was an untimely diagnosis, to be honest, because I was about to be put under the worst stress imaginable. Not long after the World Cup ended, an escort called Jenny Thompson gave a story to the *Sunday Mirror* saying Wayne had paid her for sex on numerous occasions, including a threesome with her and another escort – Helen Wood – while I was pregnant with Kai.

This nightmare started on a fairly ordinary day while I was at my cousin's salon getting my hair done. I was due to go to a function in Liverpool that night for another hair salon I sometimes went to, where my friend Christina worked. Wayne called while I was mid-hairdo.

'I've got something to tell you,' he said.

I knew from his voice that it wasn't going be something I wanted to hear, so as he spoke, I just sat there and listened, saying nothing. As he relayed details of the story about to come out in the press, my mouth went dry and my stomach churned. I felt ill, unable to believe what I was hearing. Above me, my cousin was fussing with my hair, so I didn't want to react. I just stared ahead, blinking into the mirror with no expression.

I drove home in a daze, then called my friend and left a message.

'Christina, I'm not going to be able to come tonight.

Please tell everyone that I'm sorry. You'll find out why soon enough.'

The story came out the very next day. It had happened quite a while before, so Wayne had kept this hidden, something he'd done that had now been brought to light. It was the worst time; like the past was coming back to haunt me. Of all the things I've gone through with Wayne, this was the hardest because it turned out to be true. At the time, I remember thinking, *That's it, Coleen, there's no getting through this.*

The whole episode felt different from the story that had come out when we were younger. This time we were married and had a baby. It's hard to describe how I felt, and I never want to revisit that feeling. This was something sordid and horrible, something Wayne had admitted to. I could see how gutted he was, and I knew how ashamed he felt, but he still had a lot of questions to answer, and I had a lot of thinking to do.

The worst thing about this story was that it just seemed to go on and on. The girls involved milked it for all it was worth, which made it hard on me. I just wanted them to shut up and for it to go away. Helen Wood went into the *Celebrity Big Brother* house, and years later, she released a 'tell-all memoir' bringing the story up again while naming other celebrities she'd had sex with. Jenny Thompson did one, too – there was no end to it.

A little while after the original story broke, Jenny

rocked up at a nightclub called Mosquito while I was on a night out with my friends Claire, Louise and Katie. The club was in a Liverpool basement, and while a couple of my mates were outside smoking a cigarette, they spotted Jenny on her way in.

'The cheeky bitch. I bet she knows you're here,' Louise said.

We couldn't have known that, but that was the conclusion my over-protective mates jumped to.

'Right! We're going out there to tell her to get lost,' Claire said. 'You stay here.'

Before I could react, the girls tore up the stairs on a mission. I just stood there, clutching my drink, not knowing what to do. From what I gathered after, there'd been no violence, but they did end up chasing her down the street, shouting all sorts at her as she fled. It was all in the heat of the moment, and they were angry on my behalf. What could I say?

I was relieved it was nothing more than a shout down the street, however. Anything more would have just invited more attention, and then the whole thing would be dragged up again. Honestly, I was quite proud of myself that night; I kept my cool and didn't let it faze me at all.

On another night, a while after, I was out at a local bar called Neighbourhood with some friends when I spotted Helen Wood across the room. It was a quiet night, so she was hard to miss. She didn't draw any attention to herself, and neither did I.

This was a massive test for me and of our relationship. Everyone now knows I forgave him and we got through it, but it wasn't an overnight thing. As a family, we went through a terrible time. Nothing about this was easy for me.

It's very easy for people looking from the outside to say I should have left him, thrown in the towel, and I can understand that. When you love someone and have a history together, though, it's never as black and white as that. There's always so much more to consider.

After that story, Wayne was well and truly tarnished, and even when he wasn't misbehaving, everybody assumed he was.

A few years later, after playing against Scotland in 2016, some of the England team stayed at The Grove Hotel in Hertfordshire. A few of the boys went into London to have drinks and watch an Ultimate Fighting Championship event together, but as captain, Wayne thought it might not be a good look, so he stayed behind at The Grove and had a drink there.

There was a wedding at the hotel that night, spilling out into other parts of the hotel. Wayne had definitely had a few red wines that night and posed for pictures with some guests. This turned into a story that he was 'paralytic, boozing with mystery women'. They even suggested he'd gate-crashed the wedding. The truth is, he wasn't drinking on his own that night; other team members were enjoying themselves, but Wayne was singled out for the press story. Not that he'd ever throw anyone else under the bus to deflect from himself; he takes it on the chin and carries on.

While the story was blown out of all proportion, and there was no suggestion that anything had gone on with any women, there was the inevitable list of mistakes Wayne had made over the years added to the text. It's as if to say, well, he's got form, so this is bound to be true. That hurts me as much as it hurts him, and over time I've had to develop a tough hide to withstand it.

It's true, in the past, Wayne has been his own worst enemy, he's made bad decisions, and there are times I've been hurt by it. Still, this endless dragging-up of his past always overshadows anything wonderful and positive about him. Things that people rarely talk about – his talent, his record with Manchester United and England, and what a great father he is.

It happened for years. In 2016, I got into the car with Talk Sport on the radio – as it almost always was. Kai was in the car with me at the time, and the commentator was talking to fans who were explaining why they'd booed Wayne during England's 2–0 victory over Malta at Wembley the previous Saturday. Wayne had been under pressure as both Manchester United and England hadn't been at their best recently. I was so angry, hearing all this negativity, especially with Kai in the car hearing it too. This was his dad they were bad-mouthing and booing, as if it was all his fault. When I got home later, I took to Twitter.

> Love the way anyone and everyone has to have an
> opinion. Lighten up, life is short, give people a break.
> Some forget others have feelings too.

This was followed by a few smart-arsed comments and a back-and-forth Twitter row between us. I ended the conversation with *'Rant over!! Just get wound up like everyone else sometimes. Have a nice day.'*

It's not often I go on a rant, but some things just have to be said, right?

Chapter Twelve

In the summer of 2012, my grandad passed away. He'd been sick for some time but suddenly deteriorated, and as Wayne and I arrived back from holiday in Los Angeles that summer, Mum called asking me to come straight round to my nan's house from the airport.

In the Irish Catholic tradition, the whole family was there in the days leading up to his death. Times like that are sad, of course, but there's something about together-ness that brings comfort. We'd all been busy leading our lives, not always seeing enough of one another, yet here we all were, talking, eating, reminiscing, and looking out for my nan. There was something very special in that.

Not long after he died, I found out that I was pregnant with our second son Klay, but there was more sadness to come as the year drew to a close.

Rosie got sick a lot during the winter months. There was often a chest infection or something that would bring her down; it was something we were all accus-tomed to. I've lost count of the number of Christmases and New Years we spent in the hospital with her. Alder Hey Children's Hospital in Liverpool became our home from home. We knew all the staff by name; in fact, Mum spent so much time there that a couple of women who worked at Alder Hey have since become her closest friends.

Over Christmas of 2012, Rosie had been in and out of hospital again. It wasn't anything out of the ordinary for that time of year, but it seemed more serious than usual. I was booked to take Kai on holiday to our house in Barbados with my brothers and their partners, flying on Boxing Day. As the days passed, I wasn't sure I should be going, but Mum thought differently.

'Go away and enjoy yourselves; you can see Rosie when you get back,' she told us.

We ended up going on our holiday, but as things turned out, I wish I'd listened to my gut.

One morning, while we were all relaxing at the Barbados house, I decided to pop over to a nearby hotel to enjoy a bit of pampering at the spa. While I was there, Joe called, sounding very upset.

'Coleen, Auntie Ann just phoned. We need to get home as soon as possible.'

I didn't even have to ask why. I dashed out of the spa and rushed back to the house to pack my stuff. I phoned Rachael, who worked for Paul, asking her to get us all on a plane as soon as possible.

The flight home that followed was the worst of my life – eight hours without contact, not knowing what was happening, wondering, fearing the worst. Joe was in the seat in front of me, looking at pictures of Rosie on his iPad. At one point, he looked over his shoulder at me with such sadness.

'Come here, it's going to be OK,' I said, then I leaned over and hugged him tight.

In my heart, I suppose I knew that it wasn't going to be all right, not this time. I just wanted to be strong for my baby brother.

Still, we all cried at one point during that flight, feeling helpless, willing the plane to go faster so we could get home to Rosie. Unable to fly directly to Manchester, we had to land in London, so we organised a private plane from London to Liverpool so we didn't have to wait any longer than necessary.

Thankfully, Rosie was still with us when we arrived, but by then everyone knew it was only a matter of time. With this in mind, Mum decided to bring her home. There was nothing else the hospital could do, so Mum and Dad thought it was best. That way, Rosie could be in her own room in her own bed, comfortable and surrounded by her family.

While my dad and brothers went home to get her room ready, Mum and I travelled with Rosie in the ambulance. Knowing she would slip away from us soon, I was devastated, but I was so grateful to have that time with her. That ride in the ambulance will always be special to me, as will the time we spent at home with her.

The palliative care team from Claire House Children's Hospice were on hand the whole time, making sure Rosie was comfortable. They did some truly lovely things, such as taking Rosie's fingerprints for Mum to have made into a charm and taking the whole family's handprints to put in a canvas. They were wonderful.

After a couple of days at the house, the palliative nurse told us that Rosie's breathing had slowed and the time was getting close. So, we decided to have one last sleepover with her. Moving her to my brothers' larger room, we all set up quilts, cushions and pillows all over the floor around the bed – Joe and Anthony and their partners, Wayne, Kai and I, plus Mum and Dad, who were in the bed with Rosie. We knew she was leaving us, but we all wanted to be with her one last time.

It was a long night, and although we did our best to stay awake, as the hour got late, we all drifted off to sleep, one by one. Mum and Dad had been determined to stay with Rosie till the end, but they hadn't slept for days, so try as they might, even they drifted off as the night wore on.

At one point in the early hours, Wayne gently woke us all up.

'She's gone,' he said.

He'd somehow stayed awake and had seen Rosie take

her last breath. Mum and Dad were so upset that they'd fallen asleep, but we all thought Rosie had planned it that way, that her love for her mum and dad was such that she'd waited for them to fall asleep so she could slip away without them having to watch her go. It was the simplest, kindest way it could have happened.

As I sat up, trying to take in the news, my nose started bleeding. I don't know why; I hadn't had a nosebleed for years, but suddenly there it was – blood and tears all at once.

That morning, I carried Rosie back to her bed, and we waited for the undertaker to come and take her away. That was the hardest thing. Mum broke down as they took Rosie away from her for the last time. They'd hardly been apart since the first day Rosie arrived as a smiling two-year-old baby, and now Mum was letting her go, aged just fourteen.

It's a strange thing when someone dies. No matter how much grief is attached, there's always so much practical stuff to think about – death certificate, funeral, burial spot. I took over as much as possible, helping Mum, liaising with the funeral directors and organising the service.

It was a massive loss to us all, and still is to this day – especially for Mum and Dad. I think about Rosie a lot, but my mum would probably say I've held a lot in over the years and don't talk enough about how I feel. I think she's right; I'm not really one who shares and talks a lot. That's just my way of dealing with things. With Rosie's death, I put on a solid front for my parents, but she's never left my heart or mind. There was never a moment when we thought of Rosie as adopted. Mum and Dad saw her as their daughter, and she was my sister.

Several years earlier, Mum had joined a group called the Rett's Syndrome Society, where she met other parents of children with the condition, who all supported one another. Over the years, many of those children have passed away, but Mum still sometimes meets up with people from the group – they're still friends, still there supporting each other. One of the best things about having Rosie in the family is that we're all still in contact with her brother and sister. Through being involved with the fostering process, Mum knew the couple who eventually adopted them, which meant that the three children always kept in touch as a family unit. We're all still friends to this day.

Over the years, Wayne and I have supported charities and organisations that have touched our lives and the lives of our loved ones.

The Alder Hey Children's Hospital saved my life when I was little and was so fantastic with Rosie throughout her life. Children are sent to Alder Hey from all over the country because of its reputation for brilliant services and treatment, but we're lucky to have it right on our doorstep. Wayne and I have long been patrons of the hospital and, over the years, have tried to help raise as much money as possible for this fantastic place.

Claire House, the children's hospice, is another place we've long championed. Although it's been ten years since Rosie's death, Claire House continues to support us as a family. As an organisation, their job doesn't just stop when a child dies; they keep in touch, checking in on my mum and dad regularly. Every year, they even have a Remembrance Day service where the families of children who've passed away can get together, go to mass and celebrate their lives.

By the same token, I've supported the Jeans for Genes campaign for years, which raises awareness of the challenges faced by people like Rosie living with a genetic condition. Jeans for Genes Day takes place in September when people donate to wear their jeans to work and school. The money raised goes towards research, cures and support for those affected. Over the years, there's been a student competition to design a T-shirt for the campaign, and I've regularly been on the panel that chooses the winner. I love doing it because if we can get people in the public eye wearing the T-shirt, it helps boost sales and raises more money.

There was so much love for Rosie, which came from all directions, and I always wanted to share that love. Rosie touched the lives of everyone who knew her. Several people told us that knowing her made them open their eyes to the world and look at things differently. And they were right. You could think you're having the worst day, but then you'd look at Rosie and see all the things she had to deal with, but she'd still be smiling and radiating so much love. That smile touched everyone who met her.

Chapter Thirteen

Over the years, I've been pregnant through several holidays and parties, and some big important events. This means if there have been any drunken shenanigans, I've not been a part of them. Whether it's a good or bad thing depends on your outlook, but that's the hand you're dealt when you're pregnant, and you have to stick with it. When a group of girlfriends and I flew to Stockholm to see house music supergroup Swedish House Mafia on their farewell tour in 2012, it was most definitely a good thing, although I'd planned the trip before I was pregnant.

As it turned out, we were staying in the same hotel as the band's PR team, who invited us to follow them to the stadium for pre-show drinks and then later join them for the after-party.

'Great, we'd love to come and meet the band,' I enthused.

We enjoyed pre-show drinks with the band and their team, and had such a fantastic time at the show, but as I was carrying Klay, I was on Becks Blue – a non-alcoholic lager – while the other girls were all going for it. I'd been excited about the prospect of going to the after-party and hanging out with the band, but by the time the concert was over, I was starting to wonder if it was a good idea. My sister-in-law Amy fell down some stairs, one of the girls was vomiting and another was wandering around with one missing shoe. *No*, I thought, *I'm not going to an after-party with this lot, not in that state.*

Instead, I insisted that we all went back to the hotel. I'm sure if I hadn't been pregnant, I'd have found myself in a similar predicament, and I know they thought I was a massive party pooper. The following morning, however, they all thanked me for stopping them from making a show of themselves in front of one of our favourite bands. Instead, we'd grabbed a McDonald's, washed it down with sugary milkshakes and gone to bed.

On another trip – to the South of France – Wayne and I met up with Wayne's friend Wes and his partner Leanne, who'd chartered a boat while Wayne and I were on another with Joe, his wife Amy, and Anthony. One night, we were at a club called Club VIP, and everyone was partying except me – I was pregnant, so didn't last long. By 2 a.m., I was sitting there thinking, *Oh my days, what am I doing here?* Meanwhile, they were all having the time of their lives.

We ended up heading back to the boats with a massive bottle of Grey Goose vodka that they'd bought but not finished and which my brother Joe was carrying on his shoulder. By now, my shoes were off because my feet had swollen up so much, and as I marched along with this drunken posse staggering behind me, I was not entertained in the slightest.

When we got back to the harbour, I told them I was going to bed, and if there was any after-party to be had, it would be happening on the other boat, not ours. I needed sleep. Of course, they were all fairly delicate the next day, while I was as fresh as a daisy. Well, a daisy with very swollen feet.

I'm not always that well behaved. At one Christmas night out with the wives and partners of the Man United players, I did get a bit drunk. Well, more than a bit. A couple of the girls shared a car home with me, but after we dropped Lisa Carrick off, I fell asleep in the car. Kaya, who's married to Phil Jones, was still in the car with me, and although she tried her best to wake me up, I was completely gone.

Thinking my mum was at my house with the kids, Kaya phoned her. But Mum was actually at her own house in Liverpool, now panicking, having been woken up in the middle of the night to news that her daughter was unconscious. Eventually, Kaya got me back to my house and we managed to get through the gates and up to the house with me barely functioning. When we got to the front door, I couldn't put the alarm code in correctly, and after a couple of bad attempts, the house was screaming with a deafening, siren-like alarm. Before I knew it, our housekeeper Myrna had dashed over from her flat, and the police had turned up, alerted by security that there'd been an attempted break-in.

Once it was all calm again, and I was safely inside, I forgot to open the front gates, so Kaya spent absolutely ages with the driver, trying to get off the property through the locked security gates.

When I woke up the next morning with the most dreadful banging head, I was completely oblivious to the previous night's shenanigans. At the bottom of my bed I found a note, which turned out to be from my dad. After Kaya's late-night phone call, he'd driven over to ours at 4 a.m. to make sure I was OK. The note said, *'Don't worry, I'll take the boys to the barbers this morning* [something I was supposed to be doing]. *I think you need a bit of a rest, love Dad.'* He'd also left a bottle of water, paracetamol and a vitamin C tablet. I had no idea he'd even been there; all I knew was that I felt horrendously anxious about what may or may not have happened the night before – I couldn't remember a bloody thing. I phoned Kaya, who told me I'd been fine, just tired – in fact, I'd practically fallen asleep in the club, which is why we'd all left.

I have to say, that wasn't the best of days – I felt absolutely terrible for hours.

By the time Klay came along, I was much more relaxed than I had been with Kai. Things felt more straightforward,

I suppose. I'd done it once, so I could do it again. One of my happiest memories about that time was seeing Kai's face light up when I first brought his baby brother home – that was beautiful.

Klay was born in May 2013, just as the football season was ending – our holiday time, our 'let's do things while we've got the window of opportunity' time. I remember getting Klay's passport pictures done as soon as he was out of the womb so we could get away as soon as possible. That's how much more relaxed I was this time around – *right, he's here, now let's go on holiday!*

We also went to Glastonbury that year. I remember joking about what a terrible mother I must be, having just had a baby and now partying at a festival just a few weeks later. There were a few laughs about it among friends, but I knew Klay was in safe hands with my mum, and after all those months of no-drinking and watching what I ate, I felt like I deserved a bit of indulgence.

And it was very indulgent! For a start, we had two Winnebagos for camping around Windinglake, a nearby site with a few more mod cons than the main Glasto site. There's warm water, showers, flushing toilets, a breakfast marquee and shuttle buses to and from the site. There's also a helipad, which was handy for us as we flew in and out by helicopter. Those were the good old days – always appreciated and never forgotten.

This was our second time at Glastonbury, having seen

Beyoncé's headline performance two years before, in 2011. Wayne's always had a massive crush on Queen Bey, but by the time she was due to play on that Sunday evening, he was done in.

'I'm not going to make it all the way over to the main stage,' he said. 'I think I'm just going to stay where I am and chill.'

I knew he must have been feeling fragile, especially as my friend Camilla – my co-presenter on *Coleen's Real Women* – had arranged for us to watch Beyoncé from the side of the stage rather than in the crowd. Still, Wayne hadn't slept much that weekend, so insisted on staying put.

When we reached the backstage area, we could see Beyoncé getting ready in her room, and as the excitement built, Jay-Z came strolling over to where we were standing. He said hello to everyone and asked me, 'Where's your husband?'

My jaw nearly hit the floor. 'Oh, he'll be coming over soon,' I lied.

I knew if there was a chance we might get to meet Beyoncé, it would be when Wayne was around. If he'd been there at that moment, I'm pretty sure Jay-Z would have taken us over to introduce us. I was gutted.

Beyoncé's performance was stunning; seeing her do her thing at such close quarters was a breathtaking experience. During her set, photos of people in the crowd enjoying themselves throughout the weekend flashed up on the giant screen behind her. Suddenly, I saw Wayne's huge face looming above the star as she gave it her all – a press shot from the day before. He wasn't even with us, but his mug was on the screen with everyone cheering. Meanwhile, he was probably fast asleep, selfishly ruining my chances of meeting Beyoncé.

Needless to say, he was also gutted when I told him what had happened and what he'd missed.

It's funny, Mum always says she'd love to go to Glastonbury, 'Just to sit outside, relax and listen to a bit of music.'

I've tried to explain to her that there's a bit more to it than that – traffic for miles, camping, sometimes rain and mud, a lot of planning routes, getting lost and a lot of walking. She'd hate it.

'I'll tell you what, Mum,' I said one day when she mentioned it. 'You might as well go to a nice caravan site, have some drinks and put an iPod speaker outside instead.'

Music has always been such a big thing in our family, and some of my favourite nights out have been at live concerts. We even had a box at Manchester Arena for a short while because we went to so many. I'd find myself going to random shows with groups of girlfriends to get as much use out of it as possible.

My favourite shows were the smaller ones. Adele at The Apollo, back in the days before she was doing huge arena shows, and I loved seeing Lewis Capaldi there too. For me, it's always best to see artists in a slightly more intimate setting. Seeing Beyoncé and Jay-Z in Paris was also fairly momentous, and I always love seeing Ed Sheeran – Wayne and I class ourselves as Ed's mega-fans. The first time I saw Ed was in Leeds, with my sister-in-law Amy, Claire and my cousin Carly. We had passes to go back and meet Ed before the show, so we were doubly excited about the night. When we arrived backstage, Ed kindly offered us a drink.

'I've only got beers and wines, what would you like, ladies?'

'Oh, fine, we've got our own with us,' Carly piped up.

'What do you mean, you've got your own?' Ed looked a bit confused as Amy pulled out a paddle hairbrush and started unscrewing the top of it.

'I mean, we've got our own drink in here.'

Amy had brought in a Bev-Brush, which is basically a secret flask for smuggling alcohol into places you're not supposed to. 'I've got some vodka in here; if I could just have a Diet Coke, please.'

Ed looked completely bewildered, and strangely fascinated.

'This is the best thing I've ever seen,' he laughed.

Ed's security team also had a laugh about it, telling us they were going to be on the lookout for anyone bringing them in.

Amy ran through the various items you could get to smuggle alcohol into places, explaining that it wasn't so much that we didn't want to pay for booze, it was more the convenience of not running to the bar every half hour in the middle of a concert.

After that night, I sent Ed a little gift to say thank you – a Bev-Cam, which, as you've probably guessed, is a flask disguised as a camera.

On one memorable night, we piled into a limo to go to Newcastle to watch Stereophonics with a group of family and friends. After the show, we all ended up on the tour bus back to their hotel and then partied with the band. In the early hours, we were back in the car, sleeping all the way home. Wow, there were some sore heads, and because it was early morning by the time we arrived back, some of our crowd had to go straight to work. There's been a few occasions when we've found ourselves at after-show parties and thought, *Shit, look at the time; we'd better go home.* Then we've stayed just a little while longer.

As well as Glastonbury, Wimbledon was another high-light in 2013 – again, it was our first time at the tournament and the year Andy Murray won for the first time. Wayne loves Wimbledon, but I was never the biggest tennis follower back then, although I enjoyed watching the odd match, and I've since become a fan.

That day was hot and beautiful, and the atmosphere was electric. I couldn't help but get swept up in the moment – who doesn't love champagne and strawberries? Of course, sitting in the royal box with Gerard Butler, Victoria Beckham and Bradley Cooper wasn't something to be sniffed at either.

When Klay was just over a year old, he was on his way to his first World Cup tournament. OK, so Brazil seemed like an awfully long way to go with two young children, but I felt this might be one of Wayne's last big international tournaments, and I wanted the boys to have that experience. I didn't want them asking me down the line, 'Why didn't you take us to watch Daddy in the World Cup?'

Still, there was a hell of a lot of organisation involved, and the idea that we might need security was mentioned. Mum and Dad came with me to help out, but, as usual, I overpacked massively. You never know how long you'll be out there because you don't know how long the team will stay in the tournament – so a girl has to be prepared for any eventuality. Of course, this spawned a newspaper report about how many suitcases I had, and as it turned out, England didn't last long anyway – knocked out at the group stage for the first time since the late 1950s.

I was glad we went, though; Brazil's probably not a place I would have gone on holiday, but I enjoyed being there. And despite having security with us in Rio, as we'd been advised, I felt very relaxed. We stayed along the strip just up from Copacabana beach, which was beautiful and perfect for the kids.

There was, however, one quite hairy moment while we were there – and no amount of security could have stopped it from happening. We'd been out walking beach-side with Kai on a little scooter, pushing himself along the running track that followed the beach road. My dad had stayed in the hotel while Klay slept, so it was just Mum and I out for a stroll with Kai.

We were laughing and chatting as we watched Kai on his micro scooter, gathering speed, getting faster and faster. Quite suddenly, it dawned on me how far away he was. It didn't look like he was planning to slow down any time soon, either. I called out to him over and over, but by the time I realised he wasn't going to stop, he was much too far away to run after. In fact, he was fast disappearing in the distance.

'Mum, what am I going to do?' I said, panicking. 'It's a main road.'

He was heading towards our hotel, so I called my dad.

'Get outside the hotel and grab Kai as he goes past,' I screamed.

As I hung up the phone, a policeman came past us on a quad bike, so I frantically flagged him down.

'My son. Disappeared. Up there,' I pointed ahead. 'He's only five years old.'

The policeman didn't have a clue what I was saying, but he could see I was panicking.

I patted my chest, then gestured towards the bike. 'Me. Get on the back?'

He shrugged, and I jumped on, still shouting and pointing. 'Go! Small boy! Go!'

The next thing I know, I'm haring along the edge of Copacabana beach with this poor Brazilian policeman who didn't have a clue why I was on the back of his quad bike, clinging on for dear life and shouting my head off. As my mum disappeared into the distance, my dad came into view before me, running out of our hotel just in time to grab his speeding grandson. We pulled up just as my dad got hold of Kai, who looked at me in horror – as if to say, what's my mummy doing on the back of a police bike?

I enjoyed what was to be Wayne's last World Cup tournament, but gone were the days of running around having fun with the other wives, girlfriends and families with everything organised. This time, we had to do everything off our own bat, and getting the kids organised and to games was hard work, especially when they were evening matches.

Still, Kai made his mark on that World Cup when the *Sun* featured a picture of him crying on their front page, saying how devastated he was at England – and his dad – being knocked out of the tournament. 'Kai is distraught after Dad Wayne leads England to defeat.' That headline pissed me off, and I took to Twitter to say so. Newspapers shouldn't be using close-up photographs of a child as a means to have a go at their parents. It's not on. In truth, Kai was only crying because I'd told him off for taking Klay's dummy – it had absolutely nothing to do with the match. Still, I suppose that wouldn't have made such an interesting story.

Chapter Fourteen

My previous two pregnancies had gone without a hitch, but something wasn't right when I got pregnant in 2014. Again, I was ten weeks along when I started bleeding. This time, when the doctors checked the baby, there was no heartbeat.

The following day, I went into the hospital because the foetus hadn't come away naturally. Mum and Wayne went to the hospital with me, where I took a tablet and then waited. Hours later, the doctor told me they were pretty sure it was all done and that I could go home. They were wrong, as it turned out.

The next morning, I was on the toilet, and the foetus finally came away. It was a shock, and I had no idea what to do. The doctors had said it was gone, but here it was. I didn't know what to do. Was I supposed to call someone, tell a doctor? I was unsure, but felt OK, and I don't think there was anything the hospital could have done, so I just left it.

It's devastating when something like this happens; of course it is. My feelings about it this time were slightly different, though. I knew I had two healthy boys and that I'd most likely be able to have another when the time was right. I wasn't as nervous going forward.

I've wondered since if I could only have boys, that I couldn't carry girls and that the two I lost might have been female. Mum says maybe I'm just meant to be the mum of boys, and that's fine by me.

With having children, the change from two to three was the biggest. With two kids, Wayne and I had one-a-piece to deal with at any given time, but with the arrival of our third, Kit, things were a lot trickier. We had, and still have, wonderful childcare assistance from a fantastic lady, Jo. She was and is a godsend, but life generally felt more hectic with three.

2016 wasn't my favourite year. Following Kit's birth, coming up to my thirtieth birthday, I felt this creeping anxiety. It wasn't something that I'd been worrying about for ages, but suddenly there it was. I have since spoken to other friends about this, and I think it's pretty standard, that slight panic about the passing of time approaching a milestone birthday. Not that I think thirty is old – it's not – but while I was on holiday a couple of weeks before the big day, I found myself fretting about the future and stressing about the kids a bit more than usual. I felt itchy about my career and whether I even had one after having the boys. I guess I was overthinking everything, but it was unsettling and not something I felt I could talk to anyone about.

In the August of that year, Wayne was granted a testimonial match, recognising twelve years at Man United. That night, 60,000 people were at Old Trafford to watch the home side draw 0–0 with Everton. The match raised an incredible 1.2 million pounds for Wayne's charity foundation for disadvantaged children, but for us, that fantastic night ended on a dark note.

For a long time, we've had the most wonderful live-in housekeepers, Myrna and Rodrigo – a couple who've been with us for thirteen years now, and back then, they had their own private apartment built above the garages of the house. Myrna was in charge of the house, and Rodrigo looked after the grounds.

Over the years, we've invited Myrna and Rodrigo to various things, but they always preferred to stay at home and take care of the house while we were out. Still, with Wayne's testimonial being such a special occasion, they decided to come with us that night, and we were made up that they'd accepted. This would be a wonderful family night for us all to enjoy.

Ian and Andy, our house maintenance guys, were also at the stadium. Towards the end of the game, Ian came to our box and told me he'd got a call from the police.

'Why, what's happened?' my blood ran cold.

'They think somebody's tried to break in,' he told me. 'Don't worry, it's being dealt with; you don't have to leave the game.'

Ian then went over to the house with one of the Man United security team.

By the time we arrived home, there were police all over the house – and so many. I wasn't keen on looking through the security camera footage with them at first, but after a while I went into the room anyway. Looking at the footage, I could clearly see a man walking in the garden and looking around for a potential way in. The police had been alerted by our security system, and got there as fast as they could, almost catching him. In his haste to get away he'd left a backpack containing cable ties and a balaclava, which terrified me. Whatever this guy was doing there, he clearly had thoughts or plans to do something terrible. I thought about what might have happened if someone had been there and tried to tackle him. I said a silent prayer and thanked God that it had happened on the one night when Myrna and Rodrigo had agreed to come out with us rather than staying home to keep an eye on things. I dread to think what might have happened if he'd broken in and they'd been there.

Luckily, as he was peering through one of the windows, he'd breathed on a glass pane, leaving DNA. There was also DNA on his balaclava, which matched that on the glass. As well as that, his car registration was picked up on the security camera. His name was Robert McNamara, a former serviceman seemingly obsessed with Wayne. Motorway CCTV showed he'd twice driven all the way from Scarborough to our house, a 240-mile round trip. After his arrest, police searched his house, finding Google Maps of the area and our house. They also found a second rucksack containing a ski mask with black tape over it. Hearing all that made me go cold, thinking about what might have happened.

In court, he admitted trying to break in and was jailed for two years and eight months. Still, knowing he'd planned this for a while was unnerving. We had relatively high security at our place, so the idea that someone would try to get past all that and access our home made me very uneasy.

Before I'd had the kids, I always went to Mum and Dad's place when Wayne was away, but since having the boys, I've tended to stay put – not wanting the upheaval of packing up and going just because Wayne wasn't there. I got used to it after a while, but after the attempted break-in, I was a bit shaky again. I was particularly nervous when Wayne was involved in a match that had been widely publicised. Players' houses had often been targeted by thieves when it was known they had a game on – sometimes the houses were empty, but sometimes not. Friends of mine, Hayley and Darren Fletcher, had a break-in while Hayley was in the house, and Darren was out of the country for a Champions League match. A similar thing happened to Steven Gerrard's wife, Alex Curran, in 2007.

Over the years, we haven't had too many scares like this, but one incident really shook me up. It happened after there'd been rumours of Wayne transferring from Manchester United. During training one day, a staff member at the club warned Wayne that a group of hardcore supporters were planning to turn up at the house to protest. Kai was only a baby then, and while I was concerned, Wayne was convinced it wouldn't happen.

While standing in the kitchen that evening, I noticed something on one of the security cameras. A car pulled up outside the gate and a group of men wearing black balaclavas jumped out of it. Then another car pulled up, and then another – more men in balaclavas. I watched in horror as the guys started scaling the walls and looking into the garden. Panicking, I ran upstairs and locked myself in the bedroom with Kai. When Wayne dashed upstairs after us, I asked him what the hell was going on out there.

'It's happening; these supporters are here to protest,' he said.

'Protest? They're climbing up the friggin' wall.' I was in a real state of anxiety by now.

What if they'd got over the wall by now? What if they reached the house?

It wasn't long before the police arrived, but one of the police officers buzzed the door and spoke to Wayne rather than making them leave.

'They just want to talk to you, Mr Rooney,' he said.

'Er . . . they're wearing balaclavas,' I pointed out. 'You're not going out there.'

I was stunned by this policeman's suggestion that Wayne should pop out for a cosy chat with the men scaling our walls – what was he thinking?

Eventually, the men were dispersed. The funny thing was that there'd also been a press photographer there, capturing the moment. Someone had obviously had a tip-off, but instead of reporting what could have been a dangerous situation, they just turned up to take photos of it.

Living behind gates and worrying about having security everywhere was a pain sometimes, but when this kind of thing happened, I was glad of it.

Chapter Fifteen

I always thought I'd have three kids; that was the family I'd pictured, the number I'd set in my head. After having Kit, I was still young, not yet thirty, so my mindset shifted. I felt I had more to give, and as we were in such a privileged position as a family, I wondered if I might regret not having a fourth. The thought started as a tiny niggle in my mind, then grew and grew until I couldn't stop thinking about it. Eventually, I was sure I wanted another child and it was something we should do sooner rather than later. I also knew that four would definitely be enough; there'd be no more after that.

There are eighteen months between me and my brother Joe and sixteen between Joe and Anthony. Mum went from having no kids to three in three years, which was quite a feat in my book. While I was always excited about the idea of a new baby, I never loved being pregnant, but just got on with it. Mum, on the other hand, loved being pregnant, so during my pregnancies, whenever I had a little moan, she'd remind me of that fact.

With my brothers and I being so close in age, we've always been very close as siblings. Their partners are gorgeous girls, inside and out, and we've all become a close-knit group with our respective friends, which is how it should be. Joe's eldest, Bobby, is the same age as Kit – there's only seven weeks' difference, and they're inseparable. If they're not actually in the same room, they're on Facetime or Play-Station together. The trouble is, like many kids, they either love each other or try to kill each other, depending on the occasion, so that can sometimes be a battle. There have been times when Joe and I have had to tear them apart.

It's part and parcel of boys growing up, and it was the same for Joe and Anthony when they were little. We all had our moments, but generally speaking, we've always got on.

Joe and I are very similar – a lot of people say it. We're both energetic, enthusiastic types who like to organise – although Joe was more academically gifted than I was at school. He could pick up an exam paper and whip through it while I'd have to revise for weeks and weeks on end. We're also quite fiery when we have to be, whereas Anthony is slightly gentler and more laid back. He's into his fitness, running marathons and cycling. Anthony is one of those fantastic people who sets his mind on something and then focuses hard until he achieves it.

I'm grateful for my friendship with my brothers, but like in all families, there are times when we don't get on – especially with Joe and me being quite highly strung at times. Not long after I'd had Kai, I was at Mum and Dad's when Joe arrived, having been to McDonald's. I can't remember what we started arguing about that night; all I know is that it reached the point where I grabbed a milk-shake off his food tray and chucked it at him. It went all over him and all over the kitchen. It's funny look-ing back at it now, but I must have been fuming at the time. The good news is that we've never had the kind of fallings-out where we don't speak to one another for months or even years. You hear that happening in some families, which always strikes me as sad.

When I eventually got pregnant with Cass, I remem-ber a few friends and family members raising an eyebrow. It was a case of, *Oh my, that's a lot of kids – and what if it's another boy?* Which, of course, it was. After three boys, people imagined I must be desperate for a girl, but I really wasn't. I thought it might have been nice, but I was more concerned with having a healthy, happy child, whatever the sex. If anything, Wayne was the one who wanted a girl. I just wanted one more child to complete the family.

While carrying Cass, I went to Majorca with my mum, dad and the kids while Wayne stayed in the UK. On the last night of our trip, Wayne phoned and told me he was going out for a drink with a mate locally.

I said what I always say, 'Just make sure you message me when you get home.'

I had a feeling something was up that day. As I've said, Wayne can bottle up his feelings to the point where they'll boil over, and he'll think *'Fuck it'* – then have a blow-out. I can often sense this coming with Wayne, even long distance, and that day was one of those times. It's something about the way he talks to me. I might say something as innocent as 'just be careful,' and he'll suddenly get really arrogant, as if no one should tell him how to be, not even me. That night, he seemed determined he was going out to have a skinful, and nothing would stop him.

I went to bed with this premonition of something terrible happening. It took me ages to get off to sleep, but eventually I drifted off. In the early hours, I woke up and checked my phone. Nothing. No call from Wayne. I sat up in bed and called him, but there was no answer. I called the friend he'd gone out with, who answered but sounded like he'd had a few drinks himself. I couldn't get much sense out of him, but I discovered that Wayne was no longer with him, and he had no idea where he had gone. Now I was worried, not knowing if Wayne was crashed out at home or still out somewhere, wandering around, incommunicado.

I went back to sleep, but the next morning, I called Paul when I still couldn't get hold of him.

'I can't find Wayne. He went out last night, but I think there's something wrong.'

'Let me have a ring round,' Paul said. 'I'll find him.'

Paul did find him, but when he phoned me back to tell me where it didn't exactly come as a relief.

'He's been arrested, Coleen.'

'He's what?' My heart was in my throat, but there was a voice inside me saying, *I knew it! I bloody knew something was going to happen*. 'What for?'

At that point, it was all bits and pieces of hearsay; Paul had heard from one person who'd heard bits from somebody else.

'I'm going to get in touch with the police station and find out,' Paul said.

And off he went, leaving me fraught and trying to work out how I was going to pull myself together and get us all home.

As the morning went on, it got worse. My brother Joe phoned and told me he'd heard from a mutual friend that the police had pulled Wayne over while he was driving; he'd been drinking, and there was a woman with him.

I just felt empty. Not again, please, not more of this. I told Mum and Dad, who were understandably upset, and then I got the kids ready to leave for the airport. On the way there, my mind was all over the place, wondering what might have been going on, but until I had the details, I would just have to grit my teeth and get us home.

While I was at the airport, Wayne phoned from a car, having just left the police station.

'I'm gutted, and I'm sorry,' he said. 'Nothing happened; I just felt angry and frustrated and went off on one.'

'Why? Why do you always put yourself in these stupid situations?'

I wondered if anyone he'd been out with had seen what was happening and could have stepped in. Wayne has some great friends, but I feel there are differences in how he is with his mates to how I am with mine. I don't think lads always look after one another on a night out in the same way girls do, although I'm sure it's not the same for all men.

If I'm out, or even at one of my friends' houses, my mates will always make sure I get home safely. It's always been the same. Back when I was younger, I wasn't allowed to go clubbing unless my dad could come and pick me up at the end of the night. He'd turn up at Barcelona, the club we used to frequent back in the day, my girlfriends would pile in, and he'd drop them all off at their houses. Since then, my friends have always retained that sense of looking after one another on a night out. They're especially cautious with me, being in the public eye. There have been times when they've left their own houses and travelled in a cab to my house and back again so I don't have to jump in a random taxi alone. If I get drunk, someone will be there to look after me, and that goes both ways. Wayne has a lot of good people around him, they're good lads, but there have been times when I've wished someone had stepped in and said, 'Come on, mate, you've had enough'?

However, I don't think anyone could have stopped him on that particular night – not even the closest of friends. He'd been on a mission. I knew why he'd gone out and got drunk; Wayne drinks to be invisible. If he's enjoying himself at a family party, it's all fine because he's amongst friends, but if he's in public having a drink, that's where it can sometimes go wrong. If there's too much going on in his head, he'll drink to blot it all out and disappear from the world. What happens, of course, is the opposite. He's likely to do or say things in those situations because he's not in control. So, while he's drinking to hide, he's feeding the fire, bolstering this image that the media are pushing.

That night was one of those occasions, but as much as I knew all that, this really knocked me for six. Wayne said he didn't understand why he got in the car with a random woman, but to my mind, there was obviously an intention behind it. It left me wondering what might have happened if the police hadn't pulled them over, and that's something I've had to accept and live with.

Through various friends and contacts and one person knowing another, I found out the identity of the girl in the car – Laura Simpson. Within an hour of finding out who she was, I had a phone number and a choice. Do I ring her? Should I get the story from her side? I'd never done that sort of thing before, but I decided I wanted to know the truth. I needed to know. Still, I didn't tell anyone what I was planning. I knew if I did, someone would try to dissuade me or put doubts in my mind. For this, I needed to go with my gut.

I phoned her and recorded the call. The surprise was how matter-of-fact she was about the whole thing.

'No, there was nothing to it. I was going home, and he was getting a taxi, and we just ended up in the car together,' she told me.

There was no arguing between the two of us, and as angry as I was, I didn't shout or scream at her. I just wanted to hear her out, which I did. I never did anything with the recording; it was just for my peace of mind.

I was hit hard by it. Wayne and I had had our troubles over the years, and there had been moments when I'd had to stop and think about whether it was worth carrying on. In the past, I'd always come to the decision it was, but this felt like a step too far.

I'll be honest; I didn't know what to do. I'm not someone who makes sudden decisions but I'd had enough; I felt sickened by it all. Now I had to decide what I wanted going forward, and I needed to do that away from Wayne.

'I just can't be with you anymore,' I told him. 'I just can't see how our marriage is going to work.'

I packed bags for the kids and me and went to stay with my mum and dad. My mind was all over the place, and I needed to let things settle so I could process what had happened and then make a calm, considered decision at the end of it. Whatever that meant.

When something like that happens so publicly, there are always plenty of people who believe they know what's best, and they're never shy in voicing their opinions. There were discussions about what I should or shouldn't do in the press and on TV talk shows. It's one of the downsides of being in the public eye, and over the years, I've learned to ignore it. The people I listen to are the ones who are close to me, and that's enough.

That said, there are pros and cons when it comes to having a famous husband. Generally, I know where he's been and what he's doing. If you're an average couple and your husband's having an affair with the woman down the road or at work, you might never find out. It's much harder to hide when photographers lurk around every corner with eyes on everything you do. Of course, it's not so nice having it all splashed across the front pages. As I said, pros and cons.

This was hard, though. Through all the mistakes Wayne has made, including this one, there wasn't one single time when I thought he didn't love me. I knew the bad choices he's made and even that he'd lied to me. But I knew he loved me. Every time something has gone wrong, it's been a stupid, drunken spur-of-the-moment thing. It's been vulnerability mixed with alcohol and someone paying him attention; nothing to do with love or even affection for someone else. In the past, the knowledge of that had gotten me through. This time, I wasn't sure it was enough.

In the weeks following, Laura told her story in various salacious press articles. At first, she stuck to her story in the press that nothing had happened, but the more attention the story got, the more titbits she dropped – *Wayne said this to me, and then this happened.* Then she appeared on *This Morning*, insisting she'd been misquoted.

It took me a long time to decide to try again with Wayne. For it to work, there were going to have to be changes. He was about to be a dad again – a father of four – and I didn't want our children, our boys, to have that kind of example set, especially when Wayne has so many wonderful qualities they could learn from and adopt.

In the future, there might be times when they'll ask questions about all this, and I'll answer them honestly. We try to never keep anything from the kids because if you have secrets or hide things and they find out, it will hit them harder than if you were open and honest about it from the start.

If there are questions about what their dad has done in the past, I want them to know the rights and wrongs about certain kinds of behaviour, so they can learn from it and become better men.

Even now, I tell them, 'If you do something wrong or make a mistake, just hold your hands up and admit it. The more you hold on to something, the worse it gets.'

There was a situation with Kai some years ago where he'd made a prank call to another boy on the school bus.

He knew he'd done wrong and called me immediately, admitting what he'd done. Now he was worried because the boy's parents were going up to the school the following day to find out what had happened.

'Well, you shouldn't have done it, so when you get to school tomorrow, you go straight to your teacher and tell her what you've done,' I said. 'Then she'll deal with it, but she'll know you're sorry.'

The next day, Kai did just that. When he came home from school, he told me how much better he felt, having got it off his chest, not having to sit there waiting to be hauled in to see the teacher when the boy's parents arrived.

It's the opposite of how Wayne has sometimes dealt with things over the years. He'll hold on to things, and by the time they come out, he's got no control over the narrative. It might be something that's not even that serious, but if you don't tell the story your way, then someone else has always got the chance to tell it their way.

I try not to engage too much in other people's opinions, but I've sometimes seen comments about me that hurt. *'Coleen's a doormat, a pushover; she's got no self-respect.'* The people writing those comments don't know what's going on behind closed doors or how or why I've worked through things with Wayne. I know him through and through. I know how hard he finds certain aspects of his career and being in the limelight; the depression he's suffered because of it.

Anyone who knows me will tell you that being a door-mat and pushover is very far from my truth. If you were to ask Wayne who wears the trousers in our house, he'd tell you it was me without blinking. As would anyone who knows us.

People might say, 'Until the next time,' but I have to believe now that there isn't going to be a next time. That he's learned his lesson. For me, that's the only way forward.

Chapter Sixteen

So here we are, back where I started this book. The leaks from my private account that began while I was staying with Mum and Dad, trying to work through my marital troubles in 2017. That small spark of events that led up to the media frenzy that eventually became known as 'Wagatha Christie'. It all started then.

During that time, Wayne was back playing for his old club, Everton, where he scored his 200th Premier League goal in a 1–1 draw against Manchester City – only the second player to achieve that milestone after Alan Shearer. He'd been there for about a year when he got an offer to play for an American major league soccer team, DC United, in Washington. That was summer 2018.

Straight off, Wayne thought it was an excellent opportunity – get out of the UK and start afresh. I wasn't convinced, at least not at first. The idea of leaving home, leaving England, was unimaginable. After I sat and thought for a while, my mind started to shift. I knew how suffocated by the UK press Wayne felt, and I knew he saw America as a potential clean slate, a breath of much-needed air. Maybe he was right. Maybe this could be a new adventure for all of us, and Wayne could carry on doing what he loves without all the noise.

It took a while, but I talked myself around. I told Wayne yes, we would all go with him.

Nothing's ever easy, though. While all this was happening, we were building a new house. A house we'd planned to move into and live in as soon as it was finished, and now we were moving to America. With this in mind, we decided to put a time limit on it. Wayne's contract was for two and a half seasons, so he decided that was all he would do. After that, we'd move back to the UK.

While deciding where we'd live out there, the club suggested Louden County, Virginia, as it was close to the new training ground they were building. I didn't want to live there and was pretty vocal about it.

'I want the kids to go to a British school, so once we find one, we'll decide on the area,' I told Wayne and Paul.

The boys would eventually have to go back to the UK and slot back into the British way of teaching, so I wanted them to continue with it while we were in America. Otherwise, they'd be adjusting to a new system and switching back again, which would be tough on them. Eventually, I found the British International School of Washington, in Georgetown, close to DC, where I wanted them to go.

With that in mind, we chose to live in an area called

Bethesda, Maryland, but finding the right house to rent wasn't easy. A month or so before we made the move, Kai and I went over to look at the school and check out some houses. Most of them were furnished and not really to my taste. I remember walking into one and thinking, *I don't think I can live here, not with these carpets*. Most of the places we looked at were grand, fussy and over-decorated – a bit of a '*Real Housewives*' vibe. I wanted something clean and new – something simple to put my stamp on. None of the ones we looked at were suitable.

Eventually, we found a new-build that had never been lived in. It had all the fixtures and fittings but no free-standing furniture, so I could furnish it myself and make the surroundings familiar and homely for us and the kids. Picture frames, candles, a trampoline in the garden, toys and games they had back in the UK. Leaving their schools and friends was hard enough for them; I didn't want them to feel like we'd uprooted them and plopped them down in some alien space without their usual home comforts. As my dad often says, 'Coleen will always find a way to make things nice.'

Dad's right – I believe atmosphere is everything. Our surroundings and immediate environment impact how we feel, and that's important to me. If I go to a gathering or a picnic or barbecue, I'll always have an iPod speaker in my bag or a candle or something else to create a mood. On the other side, there's practicality. On a girl's weekend, I'm always the one with a plaster or a safety pin, or a pound coin or extra snacks. That's just me, and I enjoy being that person. Always prepared.

This house was lovely, simple with lots of wood and natural materials, on a little street where neighbours brought cookies and gifts to the door on the day we moved in. I thought that only happened in movies, but they really did: cards, peaches, dried mango and fruit baskets. I'd never experienced anything like it.

I didn't have a car for the first couple of weeks, but when we did get one, I was the designated driver because Wayne was still banned. While he got ferried back and forth to training, I handled everything else – school runs, football games, a dash to the shops for an emergency loaf – that was all down to me.

When Wayne was away, the thought that I had no friends or family nearby played on my mind. I worried about what I'd do if something happened to one of the kids or somebody broke into the house. Maybe it was a hangover from what happened a few years earlier. Deep down, I knew I'd deal with it if something happened. Still, I was always fighting this underlying sense of uneasiness and uncertainty.

Living in America full time was hard for me in those initial months. It was the first time I'd been truly separated from home and my mum and dad for any real length of time. And while my close friends were only a Facetime call away, it wasn't the same as having them in touching distance. Mum and Dad had practically brought the kids up with us, and it was especially helpful having them around whenever Wayne was away. In fact, I saw them that much, I'd even joked how, since having kids, I hardly saw the girls anymore but instead just hung out with my mum and dad – we did everything together, and still do. If they could, they would have come with me to Washington, but they also have my brothers and their families. Whisking them off to the States wouldn't have been fair on anyone.

As lovely as some of the people in my neighbourhood were, I didn't feel a strong sense of community in Washington. Fruit baskets and warm smiles were all well and good, but it didn't go much deeper than that. Maybe that was my fault; perhaps I didn't get involved enough. In fairness, I didn't have much spare time because I was constantly with the kids. Cass was only six months old, and the other boys' school was forty-five minutes away. I felt like I was constantly on the go.

It was hard for the boys too, especially Klay, who was only five at the time we moved. Of all the boys, I felt he was the most vulnerable and that leaving his home and friends back in the UK had really affected him. On his first day at school, I walked him from the underground car park to the playground. It was one of those typical American schoolyards, all concrete with basketball hoops and some goalposts for football, and kids were running around everywhere, enjoying themselves before the start of the school day. Klay looked up at me as if to say, have I really got to go in there? I felt like a terrible mum, and it worsened over the following days. Each day, I'd drop him off and stand watching for a while to make sure he was OK. Klay wasn't much into sports then, but it was heart-breaking to see him just standing there, watching the other kids play without joining in. I walked away with tears in my eyes some mornings. Honestly, I think my emotions about leaving home were mixed in there somewhere, too, making the experience more poignant.

Thankfully, Klay was always fine when I picked him up at the end of the day, and I was encouraged and happy to see that as time went on, he began to settle into his new life. In fact, of all the boys, Klay gained the most from living in America. He had the most friends, did the most things, and ultimately loved his new school. He was also the only one who came back to England with an American accent – after being there just a few months.

While Mum and Dad were over, helping us settle in, I felt so happy; the house was full of warmth and light. We laughed and talked – it was as if they'd delivered me a massive slice of home. I knew it couldn't last forever, though, and in the few days leading up to their flight home, I couldn't even talk to them. I was too upset, knowing they were going to leave soon.

The day before they were due to go, Mum eyed me over the breakfast table, nursing a coffee.

'Are you OK, Coleen; you've been very quiet?'

'Yeah, I've just got a lot on, Mum. I'm fine.'

I wasn't fine. All I could think about was how much I would miss them when they were gone.

A few days after they'd left, I felt really lonely. Of course, I had Wayne and the kids, but I felt part of me was missing. If you'd asked Wayne if he missed England, he'd have said, 'As long as I've got Coleen and the kids, I'm fine.' That's the way it should have been for me, but it wasn't. As fortunate and privileged as we are as a family, being on my own in a foreign country with four kids while Wayne was working or away was hard. Everything felt like such an effort in those first months. Apart from all the big stuff – doctors, dentists, supermarkets, various new jabs the kids had to have over there, there were things I hadn't even considered. Like, where was softplay? Where were the nicest parks, the trampoline places, and the football clubs for kids?

The boys were constantly on Facetime with their nan, grandad, uncles and cousins, but I even found that painful. When I spoke to someone back home, it had to be a plain old voice call because the moment I saw the face of someone I loved, I'd burst out crying, knowing they were so far away.

It went on for some time. We had this large, beautifully

organised pantry in the kitchen – everything labelled and in its place. That often became a sanctuary of sorts for me. If the kids were on Facetime with someone from home, I'd hear their voices and think, I'll just go and sit in the pantry for a while.

It seems ridiculous now. The kids are on the phone with my mum, and I'm sitting in the cupboard, seeking solitude among the jars of pasta and peanut butter. At the time, it was all too raw.

As Christmas drew close, my spirits lifted; I was excited about returning to the UK for the holidays. Just before we were due to leave, Wayne had agreed to an appearance in Saudi Arabia – something to do with a Formula E event – but he was literally flying in and out. As soon as he returned, he would come to the house, get changed, pick up his cases, and we would all be off to the airport together.

While I was packing and getting the kids ready, I realised it was getting late. Surely he's landed by now, I thought. It was unusual for him not to call me or text after he'd touched down, and I knew he'd got on the flight because he'd messaged me as he was getting on. I called him – no answer. I checked, and the flight had landed, but still no word from Wayne. Now I was panicking; time was running out, and our flight was looming. Where the hell was he?

I continued our preparations for leaving, only now with a sense of impending disaster, like I'd had a sharp kick in the stomach.

Right on cue, Wayne called. 'I can't speak long. I've been arrested.'

I almost took off.

'I knew something had happened. What do you mean, you've been arrested? Why?'

'I opened a door I wasn't supposed to at the airport,' he said. 'Will you phone Paul to get in touch with the club? I'll try to make the flight home.'

'Try to make the flight. Are you messing?' I couldn't believe what I was hearing. 'All I've wanted was to go home, and now you've wrecked it.'

I hung up, now a complete lunatic. I took a deep breath and phoned Paul.

'He's been arrested.'

'What the fuck do you mean, he's been arrested?' Paul said.

'He said he opened a door in the airport, and they've arrested him.'

Paul was as confused as I was but said he'd call DC United's lawyer to get in touch with the police at the airport. When Paul called back, I got the whole story. Wayne had apparently had a few drinks on the flight before taking a sleeping tablet so that he could get some rest on the way home. He felt fine until he got off the plane, when, in a bit of a daze, he tried to go through a security door, thinking it was a lift. The fact that he was wearing a backpack and a baseball cap with his hood up while trying the door, was pretty unsteady on his feet when approached by security, had not helped matters. He'd also swore at the security guards as they led him to the airport cells.

Meanwhile, I was in tears on the phone to Paul, saying, 'I just want to go home! I can't get on the flight without Wayne; they won't let me.'

The airline had a rule that one adult couldn't fly with four children as Cass was only a baby, so if Wayne didn't make the flight, I wasn't going anywhere.

Paul said, 'Coleen, you're going home no matter what. Even if I have to get someone to fly home with you, I'll get you home. You make your way to the airport and leave everything to me.'

I couldn't get my head around what was happening. I'd barely gotten over the last crisis, and now this.

The club's liaison, Rory, came to the house and picked us up. Just as we were pulling into the airport, I got a call from Paul.

'He's been released – he just got a fifty-dollar fine.'

After the lawyer arrived at the airport and explained to security who Wayne was and what had happened, he was let off with a caution – and fifty dollars lighter.

I felt like a massive weight had been lifted off my shoulders. Ultimately, it was something and nothing but it certainly caused a panic.

When Wayne turned up, he had to be handed over to me by a chaperone because he'd come straight from a police cell. He looked in a terrible state; hair all over the place, and no laces in his shoes. Apart from that, he seemed perfectly normal. Not slurring or intoxicated at all.

As he approached, I shoved a change of clothes and a toothbrush at him.

'Get in that toilet and sort yourself out so we can get on this flight,' I said.

Once we were on board I told him, 'You can look after the kids now. Do your dad duty!' and that was about all I said.

I hadn't told Mum and Dad anything about the situation because I didn't want to worry them. Consequently, when we arrived back at our house, they'd arranged for the whole family to greet us as a surprise, including my brother Joe's new baby girl, Blake, who we hadn't met. There they all were, this beautiful welcome home posse while Wayne and I plastered false grins on our faces, playing happy families so as not to spoil the moment with our travelling trauma. We were made up to be home, but whenever I look at the photograph of us both holding baby Blake that day, I know exactly what was going through my mind when it was taken.

By the time the story came out in the press we were over it and, true to form, Wayne's arrest was blown up into something it wasn't. It was a stupid thing that became a personal dilemma, and when I look back at it now, I can laugh about it. Especially the part where my husband was hand-delivered to me at the airport with no laces in his shoes.

Back in Washington after the holidays, things felt a bit brighter, but then something else happened to throw me off kilter.

With Wayne's club being sponsored by Audi, I'd been promised an Audi Q7 for our family car while we were in DC, just like the one I had at home. I was comfortable with it, and being a seven-seater, there was enough room for all of us. I didn't get it, at least not for a few months. Instead, I ended up with a Honda, which was fine but not what I would have chosen. With Wayne on a driving ban and me spending hours a day in the car running the kids back and forth to school and to their various play dates and clubs, I didn't think it was too much to ask for the car I'd been promised – it's not like I was asking for a Rolls Royce or something really fancy. Anyway, that was my constant little moan to Paul for the first few months I was there.

In January 2019, on my way home from dropping the kids off at school one morning, I went to turn left, and a truck clipped the side of the Honda, scraping along its side. The truck continued on its way, and off I went, assuming I'd probably sustained a bit of a scratch. Once I was back home, I realised the damage was considerably worse than I'd thought.

My friends all knew how fed up with the car I'd been, so I posted a picture of the damage on my personal

Instagram. The caption read *RIP half a Honda*, with a laughing emoji.

The following morning, I got a message from Kai's old football coach, who I hadn't spoken to for some time: *'Hi Coleen, I just wanted to check in to see you're OK as I've seen you've been in a car accident.'*

For a minute, I hadn't a clue what he was talking about, but after a quick Google search, I saw the headlines announcing news of my 'horror crash'.

The *Sun* said I'd been in a car crash and that one side of the car was completely caved in and that I couldn't drive it, that it looked like a total write-off. I couldn't believe it! Somebody had seen my daft, jokey post and given it to a newspaper. Even more annoying, I'd only put this on my private account.

Throughout the morning, there were more messages from various friends concerned for my well-being. I was pissed off. People back home who cared about me were reading this made-up crap and panicking. I decided to put out a Tweet.

Thank you for the messages asking if I am *OK* …
the car crash story was completely wrong … I wasn't
involved in a crash … the car was damaged by another
car. Someone on my private Instagram has seen the
picture and is telling or selling stories to a certain
newspaper.

I'd felt like things had quietened down for a while, but this set me off again. There was a pattern to these stories: they were always in the *Sun*, always 'exclusive', always the same format. I've learned over the years how the press works and how some people develop relationships with them. It felt like whoever was doing this had an 'in' or maybe a close contact at the *Sun*.

With these fresh thoughts, I set about trawling through my followers again. Being in Washington meant I had more time to myself, time to think. This was when I really started trying to put the pieces together on who might be sharing my posts. I didn't tell anyone what I was doing. Not even Wayne or my family. Yes, they all knew I'd been frustrated by the leaks, as did some of my friends, but nobody knew how much it affected me, what was going on behind the scenes, and how I was digging deep to find out who it was.

In this new search, I noted a few followers with press connections, but most of them lived locally to us in Cheshire, people I'd known for over seventeen years of living in the area. These were people who knew my family and who we'd socialised with. Of course, I couldn't be a hundred per cent certain that one of them wouldn't do the dirty on me, but it seemed extremely unlikely, and I really didn't believe they would.

There was one person on this new mental list I'd never socialised with and didn't know all that well – Rebekah

Vardy. I knew she'd done campaigns for the *Sun*; she'd even written a column for them during the 2016 Euros. She'd been on my followers list since it started, but I'd dismissed the idea of it being her repeatedly. Rebekah would know more than most how it would feel for someone to sell her out – she'd had stories written about her in the past. Surely, she wouldn't do that to someone else, to another woman. That's what I told myself anyway.

Now, with my notion about someone having a connection with the *Sun*, my thoughts about her were shifting. Rebekah was the one person I couldn't discount.

Chapter Seventeen

I'd first met Rebekah Vardy at the 2016 Euros in France. Her partner Jamie had started playing for England the previous summer, and now he was making his tournament debut, playing alongside Wayne. We'd been invited to their wedding a few months earlier but couldn't go as we'd booked a holiday. I was a little surprised we'd been invited, to be honest, because we didn't really know them as a couple, and Jamie and Wayne were colleagues rather than friends. Still, I sent a card and politely declined.

As far as the wives and girlfriends of the England players go, we don't see as much of one another as we would if the lads were playing for the same club week in, week out. England games weren't as regular, so I tended to get to know those girls more during big tournaments. Even then, it wasn't always the case that I'd get to know everyone well.

Back in the day, things were different. For the 2006 World Cup in Germany, the FA had a hand in organising the trip for the players' families and partners. It's not something they'd done while I was there, and I don't know if they do it now. During the 2006 tournament, the players' families stayed in the same hotel, and the FA organised our transport to and from games, hospitality and everything else. It was a friendly vibe, and I felt like everyone bonded because of it.

As was now the norm, the families were left to organise their travel and hotels for the 2016 Euros, and as I'd not long had Kit, Mum and Dad came with me to France to help with the three boys.

I met Rebekah at the first England game against Wales. She was sitting behind me, and we said hello and chatted a bit. However, Paul Stretford spoke to me during the game.

'There's been a bit of a hoo-ha regarding the seating arrangements,' he said.

'Why, what's happened?'

'Rebekah Vardy and her friends are sitting in seats allocated for Harpreet, and they wouldn't move when asked to.'

Harpreet Robinson was the FA family liaison officer at the tournament, and she'd been allocated the seats behind me. The FA like to ensure security is distributed around the family's seating area in case of any trouble, and that day, there was supposed to be some security behind me. It's not something I requested; it's just what happens if there's a concern about security breaches. It makes their life easier if anything kicks off.

All I knew was that, in the end, Harpreet gave up trying

to move Rebekah and her friends from the seats, and I continued watching the game.

A day or so later, I was in the park with my mum, dad and the kids when Rebekah passed by with one of her children in a pram. We stopped and chatted for a few minutes, but that was all. There wasn't socialising between wives and girlfriends at that tournament, at least not for me. It was a world away from when I was young, had no kids, and we'd all go out drinking together. From what I can tell, that sense of closeness and friendship has since returned, but I think that's because a younger group of girls is involved these days.

It was suggested at the time that Rebekah sat behind me purely to maximise her chance of media attention, knowing that I'd be a target for photographers, but I didn't take much notice. It just seemed like something and nothing, something petty and unimportant. Now, with my mind turning cartwheels, I wondered exactly what had happened that day.

On a trip back to the UK for Wayne's final England game, I saw Harpreet. She came into the box where I was sitting, and we chatted.

'How was Russia?' I asked.

The England team had not long returned from the 2018 World Cup, but Wayne hadn't been part of the squad.

'Oh, we really missed you,' Harpreet said. 'It was fine, but it didn't feel the same without you.'

It was lovely to hear, but as we were talking, a thought crept into my head. *Ask her the question, Coleen. Ask her what really happened with Rebekah and that seat debacle in France.* So, I took the plunge.

'Remember at the Euros in 2016, Harpreet? You know, that first game. Did Rebekah Vardy change seats on purpose, just to sit behind me?'

'Oh yes, we all knew that,' she said. 'We tried to get her and her party to move, but they wouldn't have it. Then one of the people she was with said they could sit where they liked and told me to fuck off. I've never been in that position before; it was shocking and quite unpleasant.'

Hearing that Rebekah had probably been a party to this exchange was just another piece of the puzzle for me, another bit of information in the bank.

Over time, Rebekah had sent me various WhatsApp messages, having got my number from a mutual acquaintance, an events organiser we both knew. There was a thank you for a gift I sent when I couldn't attend her baby shower – I'd again been surprised at the invitation as I didn't really know her besides our husbands both playing for the England squad. There were also various other questions, thoughts and comments. I'd never been the one to start a conversation or a chain of messages; I'd only ever replied to hers. The truth is, I never picked up my phone to message Rebekah because I had no reason to. We don't live close to one another or socialise in the same circle, and our husbands weren't at the same football club. Still, for some reason, Rebekah had always tried to keep the contact between us ongoing.

There was a time when she messaged me *'Just seen another shitty story online! Can they not just leave you guys alone. I don't know how you do it! It's relentless . . . stay strong. Sending hugs'*. I felt this was odd coming from someone I had no personal relationship with. I know everyone is different, but it's not something I would have done.

In September 2017, she'd even offered me a stay at her house while I was having problems with Wayne, and she messaged me again when there was something about it on TV. Once, she messaged me out of the blue when we were both mentioned in the same tabloid article. There were also messages from her while I was in America asking how I was doing after something or other appeared in the press.

At first, I felt like she was trying to get close to me, but as time went on, I started to wonder if she might be fishing for information. It felt like she was trying to get me to open up to her.

Once I'd gotten to the point where I believed Rebekah had passed on the stories, I knew I had to be sure before I took action. No matter how much I suspected her, there was no way I would accuse somebody, privately or publicly, without absolute certainty – in the end, I decided to block her from my private Instagram account. If I couldn't accuse her, then at least I could stop it from happening again – well, that's what I hoped.

When you block someone on Instagram, they don't get a notification, but if she were to search for me, my account wouldn't appear.

Quite soon after I'd blocked her, there came a Whats-App message. *'Hi, I just wondered if I've offended you in any way. I've just noticed you're not following me, and I'm not following you anymore.'*

Straight away, alarm bells went off. Why would she message me about this? Why was she looking for me online, and what would she have done to offend me? I decided to play dumb and message back.

'Oh no, sorry! One of the kids must have got hold of my phone and done it.'

I followed her back and then accepted her request to follow me again. My thinking was, if it was her, maybe there was still a way I could find out. I just didn't know how. What can you do to catch someone out in that kind of situation?

I tried a couple of things. For instance, when Rebekah messaged me about something she'd seen in the papers about Wayne, I told her I was going back to England for the half-term break when I was actually going away on holiday. I thought, if that makes it into the press, then bingo – but nothing happened.

I'm sure some people will think, if I really thought it was

her, why didn't I keep her account blocked? I can see the sense in that, but it was about my peace of mind. I wanted to know for sure, to put my mind at rest – because if it wasn't her, it was somebody else. Some friends suggested I get rid of my Instagram or start again, but I didn't want to delete my account. I enjoy Instagram, especially the account for my family and friends; it's my way of staying connected during a busy life.

After accepting Rebekah back as a follower, nothing happened for a while. Perhaps the warning and then unfollowing her had been enough. Down the line, when I saw the disclosure of her messages during the trial that's precisely what had happened. I was on to her, and now she was on to me!

I was still itching to find out for sure who the culprit was, and a few weeks later, while scrolling through Instagram, I discovered a way I could achieve it.

I came across the option 'hide my story from' and wondered if that was something I could do. For anyone that doesn't use Instagram, this is when you post something on your Instagram stories but choose who can and can't see it. You can hide your stories and live videos from specific people by selecting them from a drop-down list of profiles. I realised that if I blocked everyone but Rebekah from seeing a story – a story that was then shared with the press – I'd have my proof.

I decided to give it a go, doing a dummy run, posting

innocent stuff, and then checking how many people had viewed it, to ensure I was doing it correctly. After that, I thought about what sort of thing I might post that might interest a newspaper. I didn't want to post some out-and-out terrible lie, just something general that might pique interest and work as a story. I tried a post with a picture of suitcases with a quote about escaping the measles outbreak in Washington. It was a bit of an extravagant statement for what it was really, just a few kids with measles at the boys' school. As well as that, I realised I hadn't blocked everyone as I later saw that two people had viewed the post. Then, once I was sure I'd blocked everyone else but Rebekah, I felt ready to implement the plan.

Having had four boys, there's always been great interest in whether I desperately want to have a girl. More than that, as soon as I'd had a baby, there were constant questions about when I was having my next one – as if that was all I had to do! Anyway, that's been a massive subject in my life, so I decided to post a false story about gender selection. Now, I've never even considered or looked into the idea of choosing the sex of my child – I don't think it's even legal in the UK. I'm not against anyone who wants to go down that road, but for me, you're blessed with what you're blessed with, and I consider myself very fortunate to have four beautiful, healthy kids. Still, as I was about to go on holiday to Mexico, that was the gist of my post – thinking about going to Mexico and looking at gender

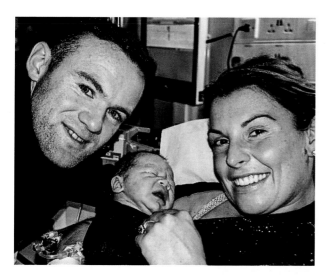

Bundle of joy: baby Kit on the day of his birth.

Brotherly love: Kai and Klay meet their new baby brother for the first time in the hospital.

Bracing the cold with Kit in Lapland.

Me and baby Cass.

Photo finish: me and my brother Joe with Kai and Klay cheering on the horses at the 2014 Grand National at Aintree.

Family business: me, Kai, Klay, Kit, Joe, Anthony and Mum supporting Wayne at the 2016 Euros in France.

Time out supporting Klay in Berlin, while the trial was taking place, in May 2022.

Chef Coleen: celebrating Cass's fourth birthday with a pizza party.

Cass and me supporting from the sidelines, week in and week out.

Fancy dress: Kai was obsessed with *The Wizard of Oz* as a toddler.

Me, Kai, Klay, Kit and Cass celebrating Valentine's Day in the US.

With the boys during the build of our new home.

Christmas traditions: me, Wayne and the kids in our annual Alder Hey charity Christmas pyjamas.

Posing with the boys for a Christmas picture at the old house.

Me in the van delivering Christmas presents.

The whole family in our matching Alder Hey pyjamas, this time at the new house.

Wayne and I were photographed arriving and leaving the High Court in London throughout the libel trial in May 2022. (*Above*) We are accompanied by my lawyer and expert communications and media barrister David Sherborne.

Game, set and match: enjoying our summer tradition of attending Wimbledon together in 2022.

Making the most of the summer sunshine while visiting Wayne in America.

Lockdown life: Klay and his home-schooling set-up during the pandemic.

Saved by the bell: the Rooney school bell which became a daily feature of lockdown life.

In vogue: behind the scenes of my first ever shoot for *Vogue*, in May 2005.

Behind the scenes of my 2023 *Vogue* September cover shoot at the family home.

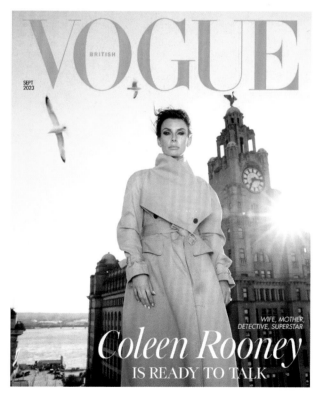

Eighteen years on from my first ever *Vogue* shoot, I am photographed for the cover of the *Vogue* September 2023 issue.

Life in the car: me and my boys.

Wayne, me and the kids
at the Dunham Massey
Christmas lights trail.

My beautiful family at Klay's Holy Communion ceremony in 2022, the weekend before
the trial began.

selection. The funny thing is, I had no idea whether it was even available in Mexico (I'm told it is), but as I was off there on holiday and could post other pictures from there, it seemed like the perfect ploy. When I checked the post later, it had only been 'seen by one' – Rebekah. I took a screenshot.

While I was in Mexico, Rebekah messaged me on Instagram, saying she was on holiday and the weather was rubbish, but it looked amazing where I was. I felt like she was hovering, but nothing happened over the next few weeks, so that was that – at least it was for now.

Chapter Eighteen

As time went on, I met some lovely people in Washington, mainly through the boys' school. The trouble was that it was hard to socialise outside of football games and after-school activities without childcare. The boys would have friends round or go to their mates' houses, but most of those were a drive away in DC, so everything I did was centred around them. Plus, Kai, Klay and Kit were all at an age when they couldn't sit still, and Cass was still in a pram. Even if I did sit down for a coffee and a chat with one of the other mums, it all felt a bit manic, and a conversation longer than a few minutes was almost impossible.

It's funny; when I say the boys went to their mates' houses, most of the time, those houses wouldn't just be regular family homes. Going to the British International School, many of their friends had parents who were ambassadors. Consequently, my boys would often be tearing around the Swiss or Hungarian Embassy on their play dates.

Towards the end of that first year, I started to adjust and relax a bit more. I remember looking ahead at the prospect of a second year without feeling dread. I was organised, the kids were more settled in their school and various clubs and, best of all, we'd found a regular babysitter. This meant that Wayne and I could have the odd night out, and I could get away and watch Wayne playing in some of DC United's evening matches. We had a private box there for our family, but it would often be just me sitting there. Not that I minded. I'd get myself a hotdog and a beer, sit back under the night sky and enjoy the game. No kids to run after, no errands, no one to drive here or there. It was bliss. At weekends, I'd take the kids to the games, but those nights on my own were special. With Cass now in a nursery, I also found time to get into SoulCycle – the high-intensity bike workout to music. It was something just for me, an energetic release, and I loved it.

During the 2019 summer holidays, we travelled back to the UK. The plan was that we'd return to America in time for the kids to start back at school for the autumn term. By then, I'd got my head around living in the States. It wasn't ideal, but I'd accepted it and felt like I had a routine that worked.

I loved being back, though, and I made the most of it. I organised a party at Mum's with all my girlfriends, we had family days out, and a group of us planned a girly weekend at Soho Farmhouse.

One evening, Wayne called me from America, saying

there was interest from Derby County in him playing for them. I didn't dare even get my hopes up. I knew he had another year's contract with DC United, but he sounded confident it could happen. Still, I didn't want to get excited or even dwell on the idea that we might be coming home, so I told no one.

Then one afternoon, while I was at Peppa Pig World, of all places, with my sisters-in-law and their boys, Wayne phoned.

'It's happening,' he said. 'I'm flying home to sign with Derby County.'

I was over the moon. I guarantee you I was more excited than any of the kids in Peppa Pig World that day. Straight away, I called the headmistress of Kai's old school, knowing how much he'd benefit from being back there. The school in America was lovely, but it wasn't up to the standard of his school in the UK.

'Can Kai have a place back at the school, please, Mrs Hamilton? We're coming home!'

For the last year or so, Wayne has been back at DC United, but now as a manager. It's a great place for him to gain managerial experience. As important as the role is, the system is different with no relegation at the end of the season. Also, with it not being the number one sport in the USA, the press scrutiny isn't the same, which allows him room and space to get on with the job. This time, with it being an eighteen-month contract, we decided that uprooting the family wasn't the right thing to do. The boys were all settled in school, with Kai in high school, and we pretty much know when Wayne will be coming home.

I'd always said that if Wayne had to live abroad for work, we'd do it as a family. I'd seen other couples separated by football but could never imagine it for us. As hard as it sometimes is, there's a practicality about how we've decided to do things now – which works for all of us. We visit Wayne during the school holidays, and he's been back home occasionally. As hard as it sometimes is being apart, it's a much better arrangement all round.

I had a great weekend at Soho Farmhouse with the girls, but while there, I glanced at a copy of the *Sun* and noticed Rebekah on the front cover of their magazine supplement, *Fabulous*. Then, two days later, a post about our weekend was taken from my private account and turned into a story in the *Sun*. This one was Coleen 'swigging a bottle of plonk while cycling at speed' around Soho Farmhouse and Claire 'drinking beer in front of families – some with babies' in the courtyard. Well, it's Soho Farmhouse, so in the courtyard, everybody's drinking in front of everyone, and the bikes are how you get around the place, so it was a bit of a non-story. That said, the slant wasn't nice, and it annoyed me reading it. While the post the story came from wasn't one I'd hidden, the timing did seem odd, what with Rebekah's recent cover spread for the *Sun*'s weekend magazine. Was she back in with them all of a sudden?

While all this was happening, I kept it all in and said nothing. I still had nothing concrete to go on, so I just pushed it all down and carried on. It was so frustrating, feeling like I had to watch everything I said or posted on line, just in case it ended up in the *Sun*, twisted into something unpleasant.

A few days later, I got a message from Rachel Monk, who does PR for me if and when I need it. I'd previously worked with her dad Ian, so she was someone I trusted. Being a PR, she knew practically everyone there was to know as far as the national press went, so I'd previously asked her if she knew if Rebekah Vardy had any close contacts at the *Sun*. She'd told me that Rebekah was pretty close to Victoria Newton, the editor of *Sun on Sunday*, and that she knew Dan Wootton, who worked directly under Victoria.

That day, she told me that the *Sun*'s Showbiz editor, Ellie Henman, had called to tell her about a story they were running about me going to Mexico to try gender selection. I messaged her back, *'OMG! OMG! OMG!'*

Seeing my slightly over-the-top response, Rachel messaged, *'Are they right?'*

'No,' I said, *'Of course not.'*

At first, I didn't know what to do. I was in shock. I'd planted that story in April, and it was now August. If a newspaper had gotten a hold of this in April, they wouldn't have held on to it for four months – they wouldn't want someone else printing it first. This was something fresh that they'd just received, and just two days after the Soho Farmhouse story.

I called Rachel, who was a bit confused by my Whats-App reaction.

'What shall I do?' she said. 'Do you want to comment?'

'No. Just tell them you can't get hold of me,' I said.

I didn't tell her what I was doing or that I had suspicions about Rebekah or my plan to try to catch her out. To be honest, it probably wouldn't have mattered if I did have a comment. If a newspaper has enough back-up on a story, they'll run it anyway. And I wanted them to run it. I wanted to have it there in black and white because I knew there was only one place, one person, it could have come from. Sure enough, on 15 August 2019, there it was. 'Col's Baby Girl Bid!'

Coleen Rooney is so desperate for her fifth baby to be a girl that she has looked into controversial 'gender selection' treatment. The 33-year-old, who has four sons with husband Wayne, flew to Mexico earlier this year to discuss the £8,000 procedure, which is unavailable in the UK.

It was a reasonably sizeable story, and as soon as it went out, other publications and websites re-ran it. Once it was out there, I wondered if I could react immediately. I thought about it a lot but ultimately decided I couldn't. Although

I was now certain beyond doubt who was behind the sharing of my stories, this was just one thing. I needed more. I needed irrefutable back-up.

Before I could catch my breath, everyone seemed to be talking about gender selection and the rights and wrong of it. I wasn't surprised to see discussions on lunchtime TV shows about whether or not I should be doing it. Of course, I had to bite my tongue. I couldn't go public with it being a load of rubbish because that would have made the whole thing pointless. My close friends and family knew it wasn't true because they knew I didn't want any more children – and one other not-insignificant detail was that Wayne had had the snip! He'd had the procedure just before he went to Washington the previous summer, so everyone close to me knew the story was bogus. They just didn't know it was me who planted it or why.

Still, the Instagram post had worked, and I had to do it again. I remember sitting down to go through the process of blocking everyone from seeing my stories, ensuring I hit everyone on the list except Rebekah. It was a pretty time-consuming job, but I was determined.

OK, so what could the next post be about? It had to be believable and interesting enough for a newspaper to want to print, but nothing that would do any significant harm. I tried a few random things – I was setting up an events company, going back to horse riding, and even enjoying a new flavour of Hula Hoops. None seemed to hit the spot, although the Hula Hoops were very nice. Eventually, I landed on a post about going back into TV. It appeared feasible – every year when all the big shows come around, I get asked whether it's *I'm A Celebrity* or *Strictly* or *Dancing on Ice*. There's always something that comes up.

Two days after I made the post, a story about me returning to TV appeared in the *Sun*.

Coleen Rooney in talks to join *Strictly* next year as she looks to revive TV career when Wayne returns to UK.

My heart was in my mouth when I saw the story, but I still didn't tell anyone what I was thinking or planning. Not even Wayne. It wasn't that I wanted to keep secrets from him or that I didn't trust him not to tell someone else. I just didn't want to get it wrong. As much as I had my suspicions Rebekah was behind it, it was still hard to get my head around the idea that someone would do this, and I wanted to understand why. Was it financial? Was it jealousy or just vindictiveness? I knew I hadn't done anything mean or nasty to her, so why?

There was no point in discussing it with Wayne; he wouldn't have been that interested even if I had told him. He'd just see it as me having a drama and tell me to let it go.

He'd have said, 'Stop wasting your time and forget it.' In fact, if he'd known the full extent of my Miss Marple antics, he'd have said, 'There's something wrong with you! You need to get a grip and move on with your life!'

And, right or wrong, that wasn't something I was ready to hear.

Despite the 'going back to TV' story, I still didn't feel ready to point the finger. The fact that I'd referenced *I'm A Celebrity* and the *Sun* had referenced *Strictly* made me uneasy.

During the subsequent trial, this post was discounted as firm evidence, but at the end of the day, a version of my quote about me going back to TV was still in the *Sun* two days after my fake post, which only Rebekah saw. On its own, maybe this wasn't a dead cert, but with everything else . . .

One night, I was at home with a bottle of wine after the kids had gone to bed. I took a picture of it and posted it with text that said, *'Needed after today. Basement flooded in the new house.'* There'd been quite a few bits in the press about the new house we were building at the time – speculation about what it looked like, where it was, what would be in it, and how much it cost. This seemed like the perfect fake story to post. Innocent enough, but something that might end up in print. Once again, only Rebekah saw the post.

A couple of days later, as I was sitting at home on my couch, browsing through Google News alerts on my phone, I saw it. In the *Sun*'s Showbiz column.

In ROO-INS Wayne and Coleen Rooney's £20million 'Morrisons mansion' flooded during Storm Lorenzo.

Oh my days, I thought. *This is it. Finally, this is it!*

The story continued,

> She was called in to find the cellar had been flooded. It was really upsetting.

The story was fake, I hadn't told a single soul I'd posted it, and Rebekah's was the only account that had viewed it. Surely, if it wasn't her passing on the stories, she must have known who it was and what was happening. It was, after all, her phone.

This was what I needed. Apart from knowing that I wasn't being paranoid and had been right all this time, I was mentally exhausted from worrying about it, inventing and posting silly stories, and blocking and unblocking all my friends from seeing my posts. My feelings were a mix of nerves and relief. I just wanted it to stop. I was so frustrated and angry at how relentless it felt, how powerless I'd been to stop it for so long. I'd put out warnings, blocked Rebekah and then reaccepted her and still, it carried on.

I always have a notebook with me; I carry one everywhere. So, on the evening of the 8 October 2019, I grabbed a pen and started to draft the text for an Instagram post I would send the following day. This one wouldn't be fake or posted to my private Instagram account. This one, I wanted everyone to see.

For a few years now someone who I trusted to follow me on my personal Instagram account has been consistently informing The *SUN* newspaper of my private posts and stories.

There has been so much information given to them about me, my friends and my family – all without my permission or knowledge.

After a long time of trying to figure out who it could be, for various reasons, I had a suspicion.

To try and prove this, I came up with an idea. I blocked everyone from viewing my Instagram stories except *ONE* account. (Those on my private account must have been wondering why I haven't had stories on there for a while.)

Over the past five months I have posted a series of false stories to see if they made their way into the Sun newspaper. And you know what, they did! The story about gender selection in Mexico, the story about returning to *TV* and then the latest story about the basement flooding in my new house.

It's been tough keeping it to myself and not making any comment at all, especially when the stories have been leaked, however I had to. Now I know for certain which account / individual it's come from.

I have saved and screenshotted all the original stories, which clearly show just one person has viewed them.

It's . . . . Rebekah Vardy's account.

Kai was off school the following day, and I'd promised to take him and his friend indoor skydiving. During that morning, I sent a WhatsApp to my brother Joe with what I wanted to write because I couldn't make the text fit in the space of an Instagram post.

'Can you make this fit so I can post it on Instagram?'

It had been a bit of a manic morning, with me getting ready to take the other boys to school, so we didn't even have time to discuss the post because I was rushing around. Joe told me later he'd been shocked upon seeing it – it was the first he knew about it – but he knows me. He knows that if I've asked him to do something, especially something as important as this, I'd have thought about it long and hard.

When he sent it back in a usable format, I looked down, reading it through one more time. Even then, I felt nervous about the idea of going public with it. But I wanted to do it. I had to.

I messaged Joe again, asking him to post it on my

public Instagram and Facebook accounts. Meanwhile, I would put it up on Twitter and my private Insta. Finally, I was ready to tell what I'd believed for so long.

After I'd dropped the younger boys off, I took Kai for a café breakfast, along with his friend Freddie. That's when I sent the post. When I left Café Nero, a few photographers were hanging around, which was nothing unusual. As I got into my car, I got a WhatsApp message from Rebekah.

Becky: Wtf is this?

Coleen: You know what this is.

Becky: Actually, I have no idea Coleen. I have zero interest in what you do or what's going on in your life.

I decided to call her rather than message back. The last thing I wanted was to get into a back-and-forth argument or explanation about why I'd done what I'd done. I preferred to say what I needed to say on the phone. The first time I called, Rebekah didn't answer. I wondered if it was because my phone number has no caller ID. Finally, I got through, and we spoke.

'I've done nothing but like and support you,' she said. 'I've defended you.'

Defended me against what, I wondered. Over time,

Rebekah has spoken about how she'd been asked to comment on my relationship with Wayne on many occasions but hadn't. I could never understand that line of excuse because why would she? She didn't really know us as a couple, so what could she say?

'I *know* who's done this to you,' she said.

'Well, do us a favour and tell me,' I said. 'Please, tell everyone. It's someone with access to your Instagram account, so tell us who it is.'

'No, it's your PR company,' Rebekah said.

'The people who do my PR are not on my private account,' I told her. 'I don't follow them. We're friendly, but we're not friends. I keep my work life separate from my personal life. Maybe you don't do that, but I do.'

Rebekah told me she let many others have her password and use her Instagram account. She also reminded me that she was pregnant. In her statement regarding that call, she said I was cold. Maybe that's because I didn't want to engage in what I saw as excuses. Her account was the only one that had seen those stories, and that's all there was to it. Telling me it was my PR company made the whole thing even more laughable. Despite this, Rebekah was still quite aggressive.

'This isn't the last you've heard of this,' she told me at the end of the call.

That was the one thing she said that I believed.

She asked me to send a screenshot of one of the posts only she was supposed to have seen, so I sent it.

There were more messages between us as she kept insisting it wasn't her.

Coleen: I'd be questioning the people who have your account then if it's not you.

Becky: Already being looked into don't worry about that. My conscience is 100% clear ... wouldn't even be arsed or upset about it if it was me, now would I. Just doesn't make sense.

Coleen: All good then.

Becky: No Coleen it's not all good. If you think for one minute I'm leaving this when you have publicly slandered me then you underestimate me massively.

She also asked me for screenshots of the other posts she was supposed to have seen exclusively.

Becky: Can you please send me the other screen shots of the stories I've supposedly sold because my lawyer wants to see them. I still completely stand by what I said. I just hope all this was worth it.

Coleen: I haven't said you sold stories ... I have
said your account has informed the paper of my
stories ... Yeh, I completely stand by what I have done,
and it's been worth it to me to find out where it came
from.

That same day, I received her lawyer's contact details, and
Rebekah told me to send them all over.

That scared me. Could she actually take me to court?
Could she sue me, or could I be prosecuted for what I'd
done? I'd never dealt personally with anything legal before.
In the past, Wayne had been through a legal battle with the
Sun, but that didn't involve me directly. I was in unknown
waters here, and all I could do was send everything to a
lawyer.

I didn't get any legal letter that day, but the way it all
happened so quickly, the fast flow of it, made me wonder
if this was a process she'd been through before.

I was in a daze for the rest of that day. When I went to
pick up the kids from school, I bumped into one of the
mums I'm friends with.

'Coleen, I've seen your post,' she said. 'Oh my God,
I'm so relieved. I was just saying to my mum the other day,
I hope she doesn't think it's me.'

'No, I would never have thought it was you,' I said,
feeling terrible.

She was the first but not the last person close to me

who expressed that same relief when it was finally out in the open. That's one of the things I felt terrible about, realising that I'd made people feel like they were under suspicion.

Something else made me feel guilty throughout all this, and that was the amount of precious time it stole from my family once it was all out there. I was massively surprised at how crazy it all went. It was all over the internet, on every news channel and in every newspaper. I thought it would be a talking point and hoped it would stop what was happening, but I could never have imagined the uproar that followed. It was like an uncontrolled explosion which set a fire that wouldn't go out. Although I was relieved to have got it all off my chest, I didn't feel happy or proud about it.

Meanwhile, with the time difference in Washington, Wayne was waking up to all this, completely oblivious and unprepared for the shit-storm happening back home. He tried to call me, of course, but couldn't get hold of me, so he called Paul.

'What the fuck's all this?' he asked.

'You fucking tell me!' Paul said in a flap.

Poor Paul. After the post went viral, my brother Joe called me.

'Paul is like a lunatic in that office,' he said. 'The phones are going mad with press and media calling left, right and centre.'

I felt terrible; he'd known nothing about any of it, so he had nothing planned. I couldn't have told him, though. I couldn't tell anyone. If I had, someone would have tried to talk me out of it or at least put the brakes on my plan, and I didn't want that.

'I wanted to do it for me in my way,' I told Paul later.

Of course, it's become a bit of a joke between us now because if I had told him, we could have had somebody with a legal eye look over it and make sure the wording wouldn't get me into trouble and land me in court.

When I finally spoke to Wayne, he sounded concerned.

'Is this really what you wanted to do,' he said, 'to put it out on social media?'

'It was, yeah,' I said. 'I found out the truth and wanted it out there.'

Wayne knows me inside out. He might not have agreed with what I'd done, but he knew I must have been very sure of my actions to have done it.

As unsettled as I was by Rebekah's threats, I didn't seriously believe my post could land me in a court battle. I'd seen so much worse on social media, with one person having their say about another. Surely, this was nothing compared to some of the stuff out there in the public domain every day. I was wrong, though. When Rebekah's lawyers finally sent a letter, we had to take legal advice.

I was told by a lawyer, 'Because of the wording you've

used in the post, it directs the accusation at her, so she's within her rights to challenge you in court. She can sue for defamation.'

I couldn't get my head around it, but I had no choice but to accept it.

Chapter Nineteen

I took the children to Lapland in December of 2019, and the minute we landed, I had to jump on a call with a lawyer in London who'd been recommended to me. By then, the initial legal proceedings were in full swing, and I relayed everything to him as we travelled on a coach from the airport. Having never faced anything like this, I didn't know what to expect. As time passed, I felt like I could hear myself saying the same things repeatedly, recapping everything that had happened, everything I'd done. It was then I started to question myself. Had I done the right thing? Am I remembering things exactly as they happened? Luckily, the answer was always the same when I had these moments. Yes, I'd done what I felt I had to do, and I'd gone over everything and written it all down. I knew exactly when and how it all happened.

I asked my lawyer about the possibility of hacking. Could a newspaper have hacked into my private account? With how it all happened, nobody on my team thought that was the case. I even wrote a private message to Adam

Mosseri, CEO of Instagram, which I'm cringing just thinking about. In the message, I explained what was happening and asked if it was possible to tell if someone had screen-shot my stories and if he might have information on whose device took that screenshot. That's how crazy I felt with this legal thing hanging over me. I tried to find every scrap of evidence I could to prove what I knew was true. Anyway, he didn't message me back, so I had no luck with that.

It was tough watching Rebekah on *Loose Women* in February 2020. She broke down in tears talking about the online abuse she'd suffered since I'd gone public, plus she'd been pregnant when it all came out. That's not in any way what I intended. I'd never want her or anyone to suffer like that. I hate the idea of someone being abused online; I've experienced how horrible it is first-hand. As for her being pregnant, I didn't choose the timing of what happened either. The moment came when I'd had enough and spoke out, which happened to be at an unfortunate time for her. Still, the idea that people might think I'd target a pregnant woman was upsetting. Was that going to be the narrative now? I felt quite unsettled by it.

It was even harder to watch knowing that, while she was sitting there pouring her heart out to the panel, she was still suing me for libel.

Over the following weeks, there was something else to be concerned about – something that would affect us all for a long time to come. *It won't happen*, I thought at first. They won't lock us all in our houses for weeks on end. How many of us thought the same thing when we first heard about this weird new virus, Covid 19?

We'd had similar scares before – bird flu, swine flu. All very scary when we heard about them on the news, but they never came to anything major, at least, nothing that affected most of our lives in any significant way.

As the news around this virus got more and more surreal, I went to a Stereophonics concert with a couple of friends at Manchester Arena. Quite a few people were wearing masks, and I wondered – should I be wearing one of those? Should we all be wearing them? Actually, should we even be here? People really were taking this seriously.

The following morning on *Good Morning Britain*, people debated whether concerts, sporting events and large gatherings should be banned altogether for the time being. *OK, so this is happening*, I thought. *It's real.*

Before I knew it, school was out, and I was Mrs Rooney – classroom teacher. Now, I've already explained how organised I am. Remember what my mum calls me – 'bossy bitch'? Well, I took my new role very seriously. If we were doing it, we were doing it correctly. I recall some of my friends with children being quite relaxed about it, but my kids had to do their work just like they would have done if they'd been on a typical day at school. I had whiteboards everywhere and various kids set up in multiple rooms around the house. Kai was in the study while Klay was in the dining room next to the study so that I could keep an eye on both of them. Kit was only in reception but still had bits of work to do, and on top of that, I had Cass, a toddler.

On that first home-schooling morning and each one after, I got them up and dressed as usual.

'Why are we getting dressed?' Kai said. 'Why can't we stay in our pyjamas?'

'Because you're on a Zoom call with your teachers, and it's a school day.'

Kai and Klay had to be on a call for registration every morning, and there'd be other Zoom calls when work was set, then another at the end of the school day. The school's system was very efficient, but I had to be on hand, overseeing the work. I didn't mind. It's not like I had anywhere else to be. Nobody did.

As I said, I was on the ball with it. I had all the stationery and pens; I even had an old school bell. The one thing I fell down on was the lunches. Although I made sure they were at a set time and strictly adhered to, my lunches clearly weren't up to the standards my boys had become accustomed to.

'What do yous want, a cheese and ham wrap?' I asked on day one.

'In school, we get proper food,' Klay said.

'Like what?'

'Like spaghetti bolognese.'

'I'm not making full-on lunches; you'll have a sandwich.'

Wayne took care of Cass while I did the school stuff, and he'd tell you I was like a lunatic – Miss Trunchbull! We'd all come together in the garden for more activities at the end of the day. The weather was beautiful, and I remember our Easter-bonnet-making afternoon being a lot of fun.

I wouldn't describe my boys as demanding, but sometimes they can be quite needy. They're not great at doing things by themselves. For instance, if they're playing outside on the trampoline, they'll want one of us there watching them. It's nice, but when you've got stuff to do, it's time-consuming with four of them. During the lockdown when they were home every day, it was exhausting.

As time passed, children who met specific criteria were allowed back to school, so I phoned the headmistress of the younger boys' school, begging, 'Please, can you just take one of my children? Just one.'

'I'm sorry, Mrs Rooney, we can't,' she said.

I knew the school places were mainly reserved for children of key workers, and in Kai's school, that meant a lot of NHS staff, people doing vital jobs. In Kit and Klay's school, some key workers were company directors who probably weren't even in the office.

'But I am a company director. I have a company,' I pleaded with the headmistress, but she wasn't having it.

It was even worse during the second lockdown when elite sports people were allowed to work, because Wayne was out of the house. Worn out and stressed by the prospect of several months being a teacher, mother, cook and playmate to four boys, I started feeling envious of those whose kids were allowed through the school gates. A friend of ours who was a sports pundit had his kids in school because he was classed as a broadcaster. I remember thinking, *If my husband weren't doing his job, there would be nothing to broadcast – so why won't the school take one of mine?* I never complained about anyone else, I just thought, *Good for you for getting them in.*

By this time, I was on my third TV. The first had been destroyed when one of the kids threw something at another – hitting the screen and shattering it. The replacement got a ball kicked through it. My days were full of boys wrestling and fighting and running around the house like little maniacs while I did my best to rein them in and sit them down to do reading, spelling and times tables. The place was manic.

When Kai got a PC up in his room, he wanted to work upstairs, which meant school was now a two-storey job. That got too much, so in the end, I trusted Kai to get on with his work without supervision.

When it was time for parents' evening – on Zoom, of course – Kai's teacher said, 'Fingers crossed the Wi-Fi holds up, Mrs Rooney. I know Kai's been having a lot of trouble with it cutting out.'

'Right, yes,' I said, going along with it.

There was nothing wrong with the Wi-Fi. Kai had been logging off during his lessons and telling his teacher it had gone down, but I knew nothing about it.

I told Kai off, but I did laugh to myself about it. He's been pulling that kind of thing since he was little. While he was in reception class at school, the teacher told me he'd had an accident when I went to collect him one day – he'd wet himself. To me, that was strange; he hadn't done it for a couple of years by then.

'Just have a chat to him; make sure everything's OK,' the teacher suggested.

When I asked him why he'd done it, he told me that a boy in his class had done the same thing the day before and had got to wear long trousers for the rest of the afternoon. In Kai's school, they wore shorts year-round, and he hated it. He thought if he wet himself on purpose, he'd get to wear long trousers for the day as well.

Kai sometimes got annoyed when Wayne came to watch him play football. Wayne would always end up getting mobbed at the games, taking all the attention away from the match, and Wayne's attention away from Kai. I remember him once asking Wayne not to come anymore.

'You don't even watch me when you're there, Dad,' he said.

It didn't stop there either. Kai told me that every time he looked over at me while he was playing, I'd be gossiping to the other mums and not paying attention. Of course, I told him that wasn't true at all, and that I always watched him – every game.

A few weeks later, Kai came rushing over excitedly after the match. 'Mum, Mum! Did you see me score that free kick!'

'Yeah, it was great, wasn't it?' I said, enthusiastically.

'Well, that's where you're lying,' he said. 'You were talking to all the other parents the whole game, and I never even scored a free kick.'

He's switched on, that one.

With social distancing rules during Covid, the construction of the new house ground to a halt, and, just like everyone, our lives were filled with online family gatherings, quizzes and birthday get-togethers. It was like being back in America again, seeing our families on screens rather than in the flesh.

Still, we made a lot of good family memories, especially during the first lockdown when Wayne was home – having that quality time to play a ball game together or make something, being together without someone rushing off to work or school or to a play date or football practice. It meant a lot.

After all the years we'd lived in that house, I'd never got that much use out of it – and we were lucky to have so much space. As the days and weeks wore on, I couldn't help thinking about people living in flats or rooms without an outside area. I'd always known how lucky we were, having everything we had around us, but going through the pandemic and lockdown really hammered it home to me. We have so much to be grateful for.

One of the things I was grateful for during the first lockdown, in that beautifully hot English summer, was Whispering Angel rosé. That, plus back-to-back barbecue weather, was like something heaven-sent – just like it says on the bottle. Supermarket trips, when permitted, were also a highlight.

'I'm just popping to Waitrose,' I'd say to Wayne, then I'd be gone for two hours – revelling in the joy of getting away from school work and having someone new to talk to.

Wayne cottoned on after a while. 'Coleen, can you try and just stick to an hour max? I can't do this on my own.'

During the lockdown, my brother Anthony and his partner had a baby, Jesse. My mum could only see him by peering through a window, but I knew how desperate she was to hold her newest grandchild and give him a cuddle.

As soon as there was a break in some of the restrictions, Wayne and I bundled the kids in the car and drove to Mum and Dad's – not telling them we were going. My brother Joe and his family also turned up, and there we were, all crying in the back garden, like something off the TV show *Long Lost Family*.

It's funny; when I'd told my sister-in-law I was planning

to surprise Mum, she'd said, 'But she's doing a roast, Coleen, she'll go mad if yous all turn up, and she hasn't got enough to go round.'

The thing was, she always had enough to go around – whoever turned up.

Later that afternoon, as we all relaxed in the back garden, a helicopter buzzed overhead, and I instinctively ducked down to hide. I was so used to being in lockdown that, for a split second, I thought we must be doing something illegal, and this was a press helicopter trying to catch us at it.

The next thing I know, Joe's on his feet waving up to the helicopter, shouting, 'Here she is, she's down here!'

Meanwhile, the legal wheels of Rebekah's lawsuit kept turning. After what we'd all been through, the idea of a trial seemed even more ridiculous to me now, but there was nothing I could do to stop it.

Chapter Twenty

As time passed, it all started to take its toll – not just on me but on my family. It was like I wasn't there; I wasn't present. Everyday life was going on, but I was hovering somewhere above in my own world, unable to join in. At one point, I decided to change legal teams, which was another significant upheaval. It wasn't that I didn't rate my first lawyer; I just didn't feel like I gelled with him or that he quite got me.

I met Paul Lunt, a partner at the legal firm Brabners, during Covid, and there was a connection right away. He understood me and asked all the right questions. I knew he was right for the case, but there was so much to talk about, so much to explain, going over the same things repeatedly: How did you do this or that particular thing? Did anyone else know? Did you confide in anyone? When? Where? How?

With so many lengthy meetings, the whole thing started to become all-consuming. It got to the stage where I no longer felt like me; I didn't recognise myself anymore.

All I'd wanted was to stop my privacy from being violated and call out someone I felt had betrayed my trust. I hadn't chosen this fight, I didn't want it, but I had no choice but to go along with it.

I looked after and cared for my children daily, but it was like I was on auto-pilot rather than being a real presence in their lives. By the same token, things often felt strained between Wayne and me.

'I'm sick of all this legal stuff,' he told me one evening while we sat down at teatime.

I felt terrible, but the next minute, the phone went – a call from Paul Lunt which I had to take. I could see Wayne's frustration, but I didn't know what else to do. It wasn't just the hour-and-a-half or two-hour call either. While we were talking, Paul would inevitably ask me to check something or look over some piece of information or another, which meant I'd be another hour or two hours doing all that once the call was over. I couldn't just sit in front of the telly with those tasks hanging over me, so I'd be on my phone or the computer, pulling together the stuff I needed. By the time I was done, Wayne had finished his tea, bathed the kids and put them to bed and was all settled in the living room to watch something together, but by then, it was eleven at night, and I was ready for bed.

Other nights, he'd come and find me hunched over a computer.

'I'm going to bed,' he'd say, but I couldn't settle.

There were times when he had a cob on with me for not being present. That wasn't constantly the case, but we had our moments. Some nights, I'd still be up at two in the morning because my mind wouldn't let me rest. That can't have been easy for Wayne, either.

It felt like such a strange situation. I'd been the one accusing Rebekah, but suddenly, I was the defendant. I was the one who had to produce all the evidence and defend myself. Sometimes I'd stop and think, how did this happen? Why am I the one being dragged into court? I think that's one of the things people found confusing. When the court case first hit the news, many people assumed it was me suing Rebekah, not the other way around. I saw comments from people asking why I didn't just drop the case. It was so draining trying to get across that I had no control over what was happening, that the last thing I wanted to do was to be in court. It was exhausting enough explaining it to people face to face, but there was so much speculation in the media I found myself shouting at the TV like a lunatic some days.

'No! It's not that. That's not what's happening!'

Ultimately, I decided the route of silence was the way forward. I had to keep telling myself that, eventually, the truth would be out there. Then everyone would know and be able to make up their own minds.

The lead-up to the trial felt endless. It was like being in limbo because I felt like I couldn't move on with life until it was over. Before the main event, there were several other hearings – stepping stones. The first was to determine whether or not the wording of my reveal post 'clearly identified' Rebekah as being 'guilty of the serious and consistent breach of trust' that I alleged. Rebekah won that, but I'd been told beforehand that would be the case, and neither of us had to be in court for it.

In a separate trial, I wanted to ensure that Caroline Watt, as Rebekah's agent, could also be brought into the case. I lost that battle too, which resulted in me being responsible for Rebekah and Caroline's legal fees.

There were days when I didn't think I could go through with it, telling my team I couldn't face going to court. It wasn't that I ever wavered in my belief; it was just the fear of the proceedings, the show and tell of it all, with the whole world watching and everyone having an opinion. I was the one who was being sued, not Rebekah. However hard it was for her, I was the one having to defend myself and prove that what I was saying was true. It felt wrong; it felt like too much. On the days when I'd wobble, Paul Lunt would always remind me, 'You don't have to appear in court, Coleen, but it'll be better and stronger if you do.'

It all felt so stressful; an upheaval in our lives that none of us wanted or needed. Wayne always told me I'd be fine, and he believed that, but there were days when I got out of bed feeling so down on myself. A voice in my head told me, *You put yourself and your family in this position, Coleen; this is your doing. If you hadn't put that post up, none of this would be happening.* When that happened, I had to snap myself out of it; remind myself that the stories would have just kept coming if I hadn't put the post up. Wayne was great during those wobbles.

'You *have* done it,' he'd say, 'and now you're dealing with it.'

That would always get me back on track and help me to move forward.

Still, I was on an endless cycle of emotions circling around and back again. I'm not a big crier, but there were nights when I cried my heart out, exhausted and wracked with guilt at the thought of putting my family through this ordeal. Then I'd pull myself together and think, *Get a grip, Coleen, for goodness' sake! There are wars and people dying in the world, and people are going through much worse than this.* My dad's voice again, perhaps. With this thought, I'd gather myself and move on, then a week or so later, I'd be filled with guilt and doubt again and it would start all over.

'It's OK for you to feel like that,' Paul Lunt told me. 'It's completely natural, and you should allow yourself those thoughts and feelings.'

There was also the fact that I was throwing so much money at a legal battle during Covid, while I had friends and family members losing businesses or simply having a hard time surviving. I'm not saying I would have just given all that money away, but some might have gone in different ways to help certain people rather than disappearing on something I hadn't chosen to do. I held on to the guilt because this was a pot of money for our and our kids' futures.

In the end, though, money wasn't the main issue; it was more about the stress and aggravation of it all and how it affected everyone around me. It was also about me not feeling like me.

It was inevitable that ongoing worry and stress would start affecting me physically as well as mentally. In October of 2021, I had some work done on my tooth but ended up with a nasty infection running rife through my body. I was due to go on holiday to Barbados with Mum, Dad and the boys – Wayne was also going to fly over from Washington to meet us for a few days. However, I felt dreadful the day before we were due to fly. So sick that, in the evening, I saw a doctor.

'You won't be able to fly tomorrow,' he told me. You need to be seen at the hospital.'

When I got home to my mum, I burst out crying. 'I can't go on holiday tomorrow, Mum. You and Dad will have to go and take the boys.'

'We're not going on holiday and leaving you here like this,' she said.

'You must; there's no point in everyone losing out.' It wasn't even about missing the holiday by then, I just felt so deflated and worn out. 'I'll keep Cass with me, and you take the others.'

Cass was still only a baby then, and as fantastic as my parents are, taking him would hardly have been a holiday for them. In the end, my brother and his partner offered to look after Cass until I was better because I was in no fit state.

The following morning, Mum, Dad and the boys went off to the airport, while my brother was on stand-by to drop Cass at his nursery while I took myself off to the hospital – I'd been booked to go in that day.

Me being me, I told my brother, 'No, don't worry, it's fine. I'll drop Cass off at nursery and go straight to the hospital afterwards. You can pick him up after.'

When I finally got to the hospital and climbed onto the bed, the nurse had such a look of disbelief as she took my vitals. I wondered what the hell I must have looked like.

'Oh my God, how have you even done that?' she said.

'What do you mean?'

'The nursery drop-off with the state you're in. You're completely exhausted; you need to be on a drip as soon as possible.'

After taking blood, the doctors told me that the infection levels in my body were sky-high and I needed to be on an antibiotic drip. They said that although the original infection had come from my tooth, my condition could be exacerbated by stress and that, from now on, I had to start taking care of myself. My reactive arthritis means that in times of stress or infection, I get inflammation and swelling in my joints. This had also flared up in the lead-up to the court proceedings. My knee blew up like a friggin' balloon, and I had to have it drained. Then there was the iritis. It was like I was falling to bits when I think about it now. Thank goodness that nothing was major, just continued bouts of ailments brought on by the stress and worry of the trial. And the more it happened, the lower I sank.

That same October, after the infection, I threw a Halloween party at the house for the kids. I didn't have much enthusiasm for it, but I reminded myself that life had to go on for them and that none of this was their fault. I'd been aware that Kai was picking up on certain things. I noticed the occasional looks; I could sense his frustration. He'd say things like, 'Mum, are you on the phone *again*?' And I'd feel guilty because all the planning and prep for the trial took my precious time from my boys. Kai knew who Jamie Vardy was, and I knew he must have picked up enough to have a vague idea of what was going on, but I'd never sat down and explained anything to the kids.

On the day of the Halloween party, I kept telling myself, *Enjoy it, Coleen. Push all that stuff to the back of your mind, just for today.* I've always enjoyed a good party. I love being a host and getting people together – that's my thing – but I just couldn't seem to step out from the shadow of this looming trial. I was craving a moment of clear skies, but there seemed to be nothing but grey around me. It got to the stage where I didn't want to see friends or socialise, and I knew my family were worried sick about me, which made the whole thing seem even worse.

One afternoon, not long before the court case, I took Klay to football training – he plays for the Manchester United Academy at Littleton Road in Salford. Dad came along with me in the car, and when Klay went to get changed Dad turned to me, shaking his head.

'Coleen, are you all right, because you don't look well at all?'

That was the moment everything bubbled up inside me and spilt over; I started to cry, and it was hard to stop once I started.

Dad hugged me. 'I can't wait for this to be over,' he said. 'I'm really worried about what it's doing to you.'

Looking back at photographs of myself at that time, I can see the weight loss and my pale, drawn appearance. I didn't look like myself and certainly didn't feel like me.

While everybody around was trying to be there for me, showing solidarity and saying the right things, I was somewhere else, floating around, trapped in my own little bubble of anxiety and fear. I was lost.

As the trial approached, once all the documents were disclosed, I finally sat down with Kai and explained what had happened and what was about to happen. Until then, I think he probably felt it was all just a silly argument between his mum and another woman, but Kai's an intelligent boy. He's got an old head on his young shoulders, and as the information went in, I noticed a change in him. I could see he was annoyed and upset by the idea that someone had been doing something to his mum that wasn't right and that I was now having to defend myself because of it. I don't think he felt sorry for me but instead realised it was a bit more than a silly argument and that I had a reason to do everything I was doing.

Wayne was also frustrated but always fully supportive. In fact, there were times when I had to dissuade him from getting involved.

'I'm just gonna ring Jamie,' he said one morning over breakfast.

I was taken aback. Wayne and Jamie don't call one another. They'd been England teammates, but that was it; there was no rapport between them.

'I'm not sure you should do that,' I said.

'Why? I can't believe she's going through with this, and I want to know what he's got to say,' he said. 'I just want to ask Jamie, "What's going on here?"'

During the run-up to the proceedings, I couldn't have contact with Rebekah. It was all legal team to legal team, but Wayne wanted to do something practical. He felt like this was ruining the lives of his family and thought it was probably doing the same to Jamie's.

'If I can speak to Jamie man to man, I can ask him if he thinks it's really worth it, taking this to court.'

'Wayne, you can't do that.' I was moved to think he wanted to do that for us, but I was scared it might escalate or somehow make things worse – if that were even possible. 'I know you're frustrated, too, but we just have to let it run its course now. Leave it to the lawyers.'

Even then, I knew I'd be fine once it was all over. Even if things didn't go my way, I knew I'd be fine eventually. I just wanted the court case to be over because it knocked me sick every time I thought about it.

Soon, it was seeping into every part of my life, and with the court case looming, I had no appetite for socialising. Over the years, we'd had so many parties. There was a time when we'd have thrown a party at the drop of a hat. Even a quiet dinner could often turn into a party – suddenly, the music would go on, more people would turn up, and that was it – we were off. I've always loved bringing friends and family together, but when my birthday came around, I didn't plan on doing anything. I just wanted to stay low and hide away.

'I can't believe you've not organised something for your birthday,' Mum said. 'That's not like you at all.'

'OK, well, I'll just come round to yours,' I said, relenting. 'If anyone wants to pop in, they can, but I'm not fussed.'

'Right, well, I'll get some food in and a few drinks,' Mum said.

A couple of friends told me they'd drop a birthday card over while I was there, but that was about it.

The weather was mild and dry that day, and as I sat in Mum and Dad's garden, chatting away with my mates, my mood started to lighten. A few drinks in, I was on the phone to my brother's mate Neil, asking him if he wanted to pop over, set up in the garden and sing for us. After that, my cousin turned up with a load of pre-mixed cocktails, and a few more friends got wind of it and turned up. What had started as a quiet afternoon in my mum's garden was now a full-blown party – going on late into the night. I think I needed it. It was one of the only times during the lead-up to the trial that I switched off for a moment and let my mind drift off to a gentler, kinder place – a place without drama.

Chapter Twenty-One

On 10 May 2022, the trial began in the High Court of Justice. Being shit-scared was rotten enough, but as well as that, I couldn't shake off the feeling of bloody embarrassment I felt about the case. The idea of walking into that courtroom every day made me feel ashamed. We were taking up space in the High Court when there were so many more important things to be heard there, which seemed ridiculous. This battle might have meant a lot to us, but it was our battle, and in the grand scheme of things, when I thought about what else was going on in the world, it really wasn't important to anyone other than Rebekah and me.

To me, it was all performance, a show, to be played out in front of the whole country. Why couldn't Rebekah and I sit in a closed room with our legal teams without the world watching? I'd asked for that time and time again, but it fell on deaf ears. True, I had nothing to hide, but why should this thing take up so much time for so many people?

'This is going to be a shit-show,' I told Wayne. 'Not just for us, but in general. It's going to end up being entertainment, something for people to talk about. It should never have been this way.'

Looking back at it all from a distance, I think, for me, it came down to being in control. Problems in my marriage and the story leaks were awful things, but at least I was the one making assessments and decisions on how to handle things. I was the one deciding if and how I could hold my family together, I was the one trying to find out who might be doing the dirty on me. With this trial, I had no control. I was being dragged along on somebody else's whim. I had no choices.

Finally, after everything that had gone down over two years, there I was, sitting in the same room as Rebekah Vardy. I was incredibly tense that first day in court; so many thoughts were racing through my mind. I found myself obsessing over every tiny movement, every facial expression. *Do I look at her? Do I not look at her? Should I look confident or worried?* The last thing I wanted was this to feel like it was two girls bitching in the school playground. In the end, I told myself, *Coleen, whether you like it or not, you're in court. Just stay present and listen to every word that's said.*

Rebekah's barrister, Hugh Tomlinson, made his opening statement.

On the 9th of October 2019, Mrs Rooney accused Mrs Vardy of being the person who had regularly leaked information about her from her private

Instagram account to the *Sun* newspaper. As a result, Mrs Vardy and her family were subjected to abuse and threats of a really horrific nature. But the allegation in the post was false . . .

Rebekah was the first to take the stand, and I didn't take my eyes off her, although she barely looked at me throughout the trial. I wanted to take in every word she said and not miss a thing. I could see how being up there was hard for her, but I hoped she realised – remembered – that it was her that brought this down on us. I never wanted it.

My barrister was David Sherborne, who was well-versed in the areas of media and communication and specialised in confidentiality and defamation cases. David's opening questions to Rebekah were about how much she respected other people's privacy. He then read a story she'd sold to the *News of the World* in 2004 about a sexual encounter she'd had with the pop star, Peter Andre. It was graphic and not pleasant, but I hadn't known about her story involving Peter before all this. It had come a long time before she was in the public eye and before I'd met her. That kiss-and-tell thing has always baffled me. I could never understand why someone would share intimate secrets about someone, especially if the person you're telling on hasn't done you any wrong. If anything, it spoke to me about how some people are happy to court press and publicity, despite the cost to another person. I also felt terrible for Peter that this horrible *News of the World* article was being aired all over again by my legal team, but it served as an example of what Rebekah might be capable of, and that was the point of bringing it up. Rebekah told the court it was a long time ago and that she regretted it.

Later, she was asked to look at WhatsApp exchanges where she suggested to her agent Caroline Watt that she leak a story about a female celebrity having extra-marital sex with a well-known footballer. Caroline replied that she'd already tried with no luck.

This time, Rebekah said she was only joking, but it went on. She'd also suggested to Caroline a story about footballer Danny Drinkwater crashing his car, drunk, with two girls in it. She said in her message, *'I want paying for this.'*

Caroline had then sent the message about Danny to a journalist at the *Sun*, Andy Halls, but he told her someone had already leaked it. Rebekah's reaction on hearing this was, *'Fuck, someone already tipped it. I'm fuming I didn't give it to you earlier.'*

As far as my private stories went, Rebekah said that she accepted that Caroline Watt had been involved in leaking information, but it was something she knew nothing about or had approved.

This idea that Rebekah didn't know that Caroline Watt had access to my posts and that she had no idea Caroline was passing them on to the *Sun* was unbelievable to me. Many people in the public eye have someone running their social media – my brother Joe does my public Instagram. Still, I know what's going on with it and see the posts and stories of the people I'm following.

I think the text messages between Caroline and Rebekah said it all – for instance, their exchange about my accident in the Honda while I was in America . . .

Caroline: Am I imagining this or did you say yesterday that Coleen had crashed her Honda? X

Bex: She defo has x

Bex: Go in the Instagram x

Caroline: She must have taken whatever it was down as it's not there now x

Bex: She's a nasty bitch x

Caroline: She's trash x

Bex: I've taken a big dislike to her! She thinks she's amazing x

Bex: Would love to leak those stories x

Caroline: She is so up her own arse

Caroline: I would have tried to have done a story on Coleen but the evidence has been deleted x

Bex: Wonder why she deleted it! X

Caroline: Insurance?

Caroline: What was it?

Bex: A pic of the side of the car knackered x

Caroline: Can you remember what the caption said or wasn't there one? X

Bex: Yeah it was something like goodbye to half a Honda x

Caroline: I bet she was buzzing. I suppose It would be a guess to say she crashed, but I could try it x

Then there was their lovely chat after I unfollowed Rebekah on Instagram.

Caroline: Babe has Coleen unfollowed you???

Bex: *OMG* I just saw wow x

Bex: What a cunt x

Bex: I'm going to message her x

Caroline: I would leave it a while and then in a few weeks message her and ask if you have offended her x

Caroline: I bet because you had that cervical cancer chat in the sun she has unfollowed you x

Bex: She thinks it's me that's been doing stories on her! Of all the other people on her Instagram ffs! Leanne Brown etc etc x

Caroline: I know x

Bex: That cunt needs to get over herself! X

Bex: That's falling out material x

Caroline: I wouldn't say that though, If she thinks you are looking at her page she'll think it's you

Caroline: If you leave it a week or so and they say you just realised you hadn't seen a post for ages then it won't look obvious x

Bex: Unless someone told her it came from
you? X

Caroline: I don't think anyone would. Andy never would
and I wouldn't tell anyone but the sun and you would
think she'd message you if someone said your agent
had done that surely? X

And the one after my fake post on gender selection . . .

Caroline: How much of an attention seeker is Coleen.
No press off of her post about genetic selection so now
she starts posting that she's in Mexico in the hope that
someone notices x

Bex: Haha I did think that when I saw! X

Caroline: Literally showed how desperate she is.
Pretends she hates it and then can't stand it once
she doesn't get it. I am jealous she's in Mexico
though x

Bex: Unless she's trying to find out if anyone will leak
it? Fuck knows x

Caroline: Definitely x

*

In the flurry of messages after I'd put up the now infamous reveal post, Caroline even composed the message that Rebekah sent me later that day.

> Becky: As I have just said to you on the phone, I wish
> you had called me if you thought this. I never speak
> to anyone about you as various journalists who have
> asked me to over the years can vouch for. If you
> thought this was happening you could have told me
> & I could have changed my passwords to see if it
> stopped. Over the years various people have had access
> to my insta & just this week I found I was following
> people I didn't know and have never followed myself.
> I'm not being funny but I don't need the money, what
> would I gain from selling stories on you? I liked you
> a lot Coleen & I'm so upset that you have chosen
> to do this, especially when I'm heavily pregnant. I'm
> disgusted that I'm even having to deny this. You should
> have called me the first time this happened.

As everyone now knows, Caroline Watt did not come to court. Despite her involvement in the passing on of stories, she cited mental health reasons for her non-appearance. She also withdrew her witness statement, so she had no involvement in the case whatsoever. Given how upsetting this was for Caroline, I wondered if she'd paused to think about how upsetting it was for others to have their names dragged through the mud because of actions she might have taken and stories she might have passed on.

When Rebekah was asked about Harpreet Robinson's testimony – about Rebekah's group of friends taking her seats at the 2016 Euros to sit behind me – Rebekah suggested Harpreet was either confused or was saying what she'd been told to say.

After I'd put the warning shot post up, there was an exchange between Rebekah and Caroline about it. Caroline called me 'a victim' and 'poor Coleen' with laughing emojis. In a later message, Caroline says, *'And it wasn't someone she trusted. It was me.'* Another cry-laughing emoji.

To me, that said it all.

There had been moments leading up to the court date when I thought I might not be able to carry on. At my lowest point, I'd seriously considered putting together a statement to retract what I'd said or somehow conceding that it might not have been Rebekah, just to make it all stop. It was only when the disclosure of all these Whats-App messages came that I thought, *No, I have to do this. I have to see it through.* I was already sure of what I believed to be accurate but, for me, these messages were screaming it from the rooftops.

There were other exchanges too, but when Rebekah had previously been asked to produce messages between her and Caroline between October 2019 and July 2020, after an earlier court hearing, she said she might have changed phones during that period and didn't have them. Caroline, meanwhile, claimed to have dropped her phone in the North Sea. Still, my team didn't get that information about the loss of evidence for months, so it was too late to do anything about it.

It didn't get any better for Rebekah as her testimony went on. When David boxed her into a corner about whether she saw the flooded basement post or not, Rebekah broke down. I remember thinking, *Surely, she must regret bringing this to court*. She must.

On the day our witnesses were on the stand, Jamie Vardy came to court. He hadn't appeared before that, but maybe that's because his club was still playing. It was the only time Jamie was in court, and I remember seeing Rebekah with a notebook and pen.

All the way through the case, I'd carried certain things with me that I hoped would bring me luck. I had rosary beads blessed by the Pope, my nan's necklace, and the embroidered handkerchief I got for my sister Rosie's funeral. I kept them on me all the time – it was quite the collection.

Before Claire went up to give evidence, I'd handed her my nan's necklace, as she'd forgotten her own lucky charm. My brother Joe also held the necklace when he was on the stand. When Joe had finished giving evidence, we couldn't find it anywhere, and I panicked, but it turned up in his backpack. Paul Stretford wanted to know what the hell we were all passing around; he probably wondered why I hadn't given it to him for a bit of luck when he gave evidence.

When Wayne took the stand, he gave evidence to say that England manager Roy Hodgson and his assistant Gary Neville had asked him, as England captain, to speak to Jamie Vardy about Rebekah's media activities causing a distraction. They wanted her to calm down as there was a lot of negative press attention around the team, with Rebekah being very vocal and constantly posting from the tournament.

Hugh Tomlinson suggested that he'd never had the conversation with Jamie, that it wasn't the case. Wayne told them that he'd most definitely had the conversation, but if Jamie hadn't told Rebekah, that was his business.

When Tomlinson challenged him again, suggesting he was lying, Wayne said he was sat there under oath and that he'd one hundred per cent had the conversation. He told them Jamie was a teammate but not someone he'd ever been friends with outside football.

Wayne also told Tomlinson, 'I don't want to be in court. I know my wife doesn't want to be in court, I've watched my wife over the last two and a half years really struggle, become a different woman, a different wife. Whatever judgement comes from this case we can go on and live our lives.'

Wayne's testimony obviously didn't go down well with the Vardys. While we were at lunch, Jamie put out a press statement, inferring that Wayne didn't know what he was talking about and that he was mistaken. It seemed strange to me that Jamie didn't want to go on the witness stand and say it under oath, but an impromptu press statement was OK. If he had something to say that would help Rebekah's case, I'd have thought saying it in court would be more sensible than saying it to the press. When we returned for the afternoon session, I wondered what the reaction would be after Jamie's press statement, but neither he nor Rebekah appeared after lunch.

'Rebekah's not been feeling well,' the judge told the court.

On day four of the trial, it was my turn to testify. My team reminded me I should stick to saying 'I believe' rather than 'I know' and not to be too cocky. I don't think I'm one to get cocky, but I can stand up for myself and get argumentative, which I wanted to avoid.

Still, it's hard being questioned when the opposition is trying to trip you up. Sometimes I felt like I would burst, screaming out that I knew for sure what I was saying was true, but I couldn't.

Klay, who was nine then, was due to play at a football tournament on the weekend that fell smack bang in the middle of the trial and, as it turned out, my testimony. He'd been playing at Manchester United Academy, and this was his first trip abroad, so it was quite a big thing and, of course, he was excited. In the week leading up to that, Mum and Dad had been looking after the boys so Wayne and I could concentrate fully on the case, staying in London. As the weekend drew closer, I was torn about what to do, so I called my mum.

'I don't know, Mum, should I come home and see the kids because I haven't been around all week, or should I go with Wayne and watch Klay in the tournament? I've got to be back in court on Monday.'

'The boys are fine with me.' Mum was always the voice of reason. 'Go and watch the tournament. If you come back here for the weekend, you'll only have to leave them all over again on Sunday when you go back to London.'

I felt guilty about pretty much everything then, and the idea that I had a weekend away from the court proceedings, not spending it with all the boys, just added to that guilt. In my heart, I really wanted to watch Klay's tournament and forget about the courtroom and all the drama, even if it was just for a couple of days. So, in the end, and with Mum and Dad's blessing, that's what I decided to do.

On that Friday afternoon, I was in the witness box giving my evidence, so when court ended on Friday evening, I was still under oath and due to re-take the stand first thing on Monday morning. In that situation, you're legally bound not to discuss or divulge anything about the case to anyone, so going to Berlin was perfect, as there'd be nobody to distract me or ask me questions about what was going on.

As soon as we left court that day, we got in the car and got changed on the way to the airport. As the plane took off, I felt this sense of calm wash over me, almost as if I was leaving all the bad stuff on the runway behind me. That feeling continued over the weekend. We had a wonderful time watching our son play, and the atmosphere swept me far away from the long, drawn-out days in a London courtroom. Klay's team didn't win the tournament, but the weather was lovely, and I was just so happy to be there. Plus, Klay was over the moon that both his mum and dad were there cheering him on. Wayne doesn't always get to go to those sorts of events because he's so often working, so it was special for all of us.

That tiny window of serenity was shattered big-time on our way home from Berlin on Sunday evening. By the time we arrived at Berlin Brandenburg Airport, I'd got that Sunday-night back-to-school or -work anxiety that's probably familiar to many of us. The only thing was, it was the witness stand I was facing, so the pressure was magnified tenfold.

Our flight was delayed, not by much, but while we were sitting on the tarmac, lights dimmed, seatbelts fastened, ready to take off, the tannoy system crackled into life, and the lights came back on again.

The captain spoke. 'We're so sorry, ladies and gentlemen, but unfortunately, we're unable to take off. Airspace over Berlin is closed for the night.'

I turned to Wayne in a panic. 'But I've got to get home; I'm on the stand first thing tomorrow. I've got to be at the court.'

Wayne was unsympathetic. 'I fucking told you we should have come home earlier!'

'Well, I didn't want to come home earlier; it would have meant missing part of the tournament – the whole reason we were there,' I snapped back.

We were both tired and now I was stressed into the bargain. Filling up with tears, I grabbed a passing air steward.

'I've got to get home. I'm up in court in the morning!'

The poor guy looked at me with a mix of confusion and sympathy.

'I'm so sorry, we tried absolutely everything, but we just can't take off. Everyone has to disembark.'

I was beside myself, imagining everyone sitting in the court the following day, waiting for me to appear, assuming I couldn't be bothered to turn up to give my testimony. What would everyone think if I was a no-show? The press would have a field day! The frustrating thing was that I'd been so diligent about the situation, explicitly asking my team if it would be OK for me to leave the country that weekend. It was silly, really, I wasn't on bail, and I wasn't under any criminal charges. Still, I needed to do everything right, so I asked the question. Now here I was, heading back into Berlin Brandenburg Airport – unable to leave the country.

It was Mum's birthday that week, so I'd bought her a limited-edition liqueur in duty-free to add to her birthday presents. While we were waiting for our cases to come back off the flight at the luggage carousel, Wayne picked up the bag with the bottle in, and it promptly split, smashing on the floor, glass and liquid going everywhere.

'I can't fucking believe this,' he said.

Meanwhile, the knot in my stomach tightened, and my stress levels went sky-high.

Once we'd collected our cases, the two of us bickered our way to the airport hotel for the night, where I took up my mission to find a flight to get me to the court on time while Paul Stretford, who'd stayed in London over the weekend, did the same from his end. Eventually, we found a flight to get us into Stansted Airport at 7.20 a.m. Fantastic! I could make it as long as it took off on time and there were no problems. Just!

I washed and blew out my hair in the hotel room before bed because I knew there would be no time in the morning. Meanwhile, I was sending Paul Stretford pictures of the outfit I was due to wear in court so he could go to our hotel room in London, collect my clothes, shoes, handbag and Wayne's suit, and give them to the driver who was coming to pick us up at Stansted. Thankfully I'd taken extra underwear to Berlin, so I didn't have to ask poor Paul to rifle through my knicker drawer.

After all that, I collapsed exhausted into bed, but I

reckon I slept for about three hours at most before the alarm went off. Then, I was back up and rushing around like mad, determined to get on the flight back to London and into court to finish my time on the witness stand.

Luckily, the flight went off without a hitch, and the lovely driver we'd had all through the court proceedings met us at Stansted Airport with coffees. We were both so relieved to be back in the UK; now we just had to hope the traffic would be on our side heading into town.

On the way back, our driver stopped at a pub around the corner from the court. It wasn't even open, but the cleaners were working inside, and told our driver we could use the toilets to get changed. Heaven only knows what they must have thought, seeing Wayne and Coleen Rooney rushing through the bar with armfuls of clothes, then coming out of the toilets all dressed up in our finery, ready for the day.

As scared and worried as I'd been about those court proceedings, and as much as I didn't want to be there, I was so happy and relieved when I took to the stand that morning. Paul hadn't even told my legal team what had happened because we didn't want to worry anyone, so nobody was any the wiser. Meanwhile, my heart was thumping inside my chest like crazy, but I was there. I was ready.

For me, it wasn't about winning or losing a case; it was about getting my version of events out there and letting people know that whatever happened, I was sticking to what I knew to be true. My story never changed – something my legal team said was unusual, especially being the defendant. I changed my witness statement once, only to add evidence that strengthened my story – a screenshot of another warning shot I'd put on social media, hoping to make it all stop. Throughout the proceedings, Rebekah changed her witness statement several times.

I had great faith in my legal team, and I built up a close relationship with them over time. There was a natural rapport between us all and trust on both sides. While under oath, I'd sit alone in a room, unable to discuss what was happening, even with my team. At other times, we'd sit in the room, discussing what had just happened or was about to happen.

As nervous as I was, there was often a lot of laughter when we were all together. It might sound weird to laugh at such a serious time, but I think that happens naturally, even in stressful or sad times. We might be around a hospital bed or gathered in a room with family when someone has passed away, and we can still find moments to smile or even laugh with one another. It's what keeps us going.

Wayne was another level of hilarious throughout. He was convinced he was the one running the show. He'd march into the room some days, making his thoughts known to all.

'Well, if she said this and then that happened, then I reckon this, and I think we should do that . . .'

'Well, I think you've got a good point here, Wayne,' David would say, always very accommodating.

Wayne would look all pleased with himself while I'd tell him, 'Wayne, shut up and let David speak, for goodness' sake!'

Wayne loves true crime, courtroom or murder documentaries, so to be there and watch all this unfold was fascinating for him. He also loves a discussion, and his strong views and opinions about everything became a point of good-natured humour between Wayne, Paul Lunt and Paul's senior associate Jamie Hurworth. One day, after Wayne had stridently summed up that morning's tense proceedings, we were all having lunch in the courtroom restaurant, where paintings of important legal people from over the years hung on the wall above our heads.

'Our Wayne's going to be up there one day,' Jamie said, pointing at the gallery of men in white wigs, and we all fell about laughing. It was a much-needed moment of sunshine in amongst all the grey. None of us wanted to be in this situation, so we had to grab any small pieces of joy we could find.

The trial was set to go on for seven days, but as the judge ordered an extra day to go through the evidence, and then another got slotted in before the final day, it went on for longer. I'd booked for us all to go on holiday to

Dubai straight after, as it was the school holidays and the football season had ended. This meant I wouldn't be in court for the final day, which made me slightly nervous, wondering what people might think and if I might miss something of great importance.

'It's fine, Coleen,' Paul Lunt told me. 'We knew you were going away, and there's no reason you have to be there for the final day. You've said all you need to say, and this is just the barristers summing up.'

Leaving court on that final day was so strange. As we drove towards home, back to some sort of normality, Wayne asked me how I felt now it was over.

'I don't know. I just don't know how I feel.'

It seemed like we'd been preparing for it for so long with that dread hanging over me – and not even the fear of the verdict, just the idea of being in court. Was it really all done and dusted?

We stopped off and picked up a KFC, and I grabbed a much-needed alcoholic tipple. Sitting there and enjoying the journey without a piece of paper or a notebook in front of me felt so wonderful. I wasn't looking at my phone for messages or scrolling through, searching for some piece of evidence. I was just calmly sitting there enjoying a bevvy and some takeaway chicken. It was wonderful.

When I got on that plane to Dubai, I felt like this massive weight had been lifted off my shoulders. I didn't even know what the result of the case would be, but that didn't matter. Just the fact that it was all over was enough to make me feel a thousand times lighter. We stayed in Dubai for three weeks, relaxing and enjoying being a normal family for the first time in what felt like an eternity. It was one of the best holidays I'd ever had, and spending time with my kids felt more precious than ever. I felt like I could give myself fully without my mind wandering everywhere. I knew the result of the case was still to come, but I didn't let that concern me. I was back. I was me again.

Chapter Twenty-Two

I didn't know until the day before that the judge's ruling had been made and was to be announced. In some ways, I was glad there wasn't a long lead-up because I wasn't sitting there wringing my hands, waiting to hear. On 28 July, Paul Lunt said he'd call me the following day with the results of the ruling. Then late that evening, he sent me a message.

Paul: Hi Coleen, I know we're speaking at 11 in the morning, but just message me if you want to speak before and let me know. I have no idea which way the judgement has gone, and I will find out at the same time as you in the call in the morning. Whichever way it goes, it's been a pleasure to work for you, and I know you couldn't have handled yourself any better than you did.

Coleen: I appreciate all the work you've put into the case, and I believe that everyone involved has done as much as they could. It would be great to win; however,

I have to remember that at one point during all this, I thought I had no chance. So the fact that I could be in with a chance is good enough for me! We all know the truth and I think the majority of the public do as well. Speak to you tomorrow.

Paul: You'll always be the winner in my eyes, but I'm going to be beyond gutted if the judge doesn't also see it that way. I'll probably get less sleep than you tonight but let's speak in the morning.

Coleen: It's a weird feeling, and I know it's going to be tomorrow as well.

Paul: Yes, it's like exam results day!

Coleen: Exactly!

That was how it felt, like the night before my GCSE results. Had I done well? Had I failed?

To be honest, I was surprisingly calm about the whole thing by then; it felt like the worst had already happened. After years and months of wondering, planning, worrying and waiting, what was one more night?

The following day, I drove Kai to a photo shoot for Puma and JD Sports; he'd landed a contract with Puma through his football, and the shoot for the campaign just happened to be that morning. The phone call where I'd find out the case results was set for 11 a.m., and then the judge's ruling would go public an hour later at midday. For that hour, I couldn't talk to anyone outside my legal team about the judgement.

Just before eleven, I left Kai's shoot, walked out to the car park and sat in my car, waiting for my phone to ring. I looked around at the bleak surroundings of the industrial estate. It was dead, with nobody in sight, and all I could hear was the sound of my own breathing and my fingernails tapping an impatient rhythm on the steering wheel.

Eventually, the phone went, and suddenly, the car was filled with the voices of Paul Lunt, Jamie Hurworth and barrister Ben Hamer, who were all on the call. David Sherborne was late joining, being away on holiday, but he was the one who had the news. There were a tense couple of minutes while we waited for him to join us, with us all chit-chatting nervously about nothing.

As David joined the call, I took a deep breath.

'Hi, I'm just going to jump straight in with it,' he said. 'We've won!'

I felt my whole body relax. 'Oh, fuckin' hell.'

I'm not a massive swearer. Maybe when I've had a few drinks and get a bit giddy, the odd word slips out, but day to day, I don't swear often. Still, this seemed like an occasion when no other words would do. There I was, sitting in my car in the middle of an industrial estate on my own, hearing the best, most amazing news. News I'd waited so long to hear and prayed would go my way.

Suddenly, everyone on the call was talking over one another, a mad rush of relief, joy and congratulations.

Somewhere in the middle of all this, I heard Paul Lunt ask, 'What was the judgement?' This was followed by David's explanation of Mrs Justice Steyn's ruling.

'In my judgment, Ms Rooney was an honest and reliable witness. She sought to answer the questions she was asked without any evasion. I also accept . . . Mr Rooney gave honest evidence.

'Ms Vardy . . . gave evidence for about two and a half days. It was evident that Ms Vardy found the process . . . stressful and, at times, distressing . . . I bear in mind the degree of stress she was naturally feeling, . . . [and] the abuse that she has suffered . . . Nevertheless, I find that it is, unfortunately, necessary to treat Ms Vardy's evidence with very considerable caution . . . significant parts of Ms Vardy's evidence were not credible . . .

'In my judgment, it is likely that Ms Vardy deliberately deleted her WhatsApp chat with Ms Watt, and that Ms Watt deliberately dropped her phone in the sea . . .

'[However], my assessment is that she is genuinely offended by the accusation made against her by Ms Rooney in the Reveal Post . . . that is not because she was not involved in disclosing information from the Private

Instagram Account ... Ms Vardy's part in disclosing information to the *Sun* was, it seems to me, unthinking rather than part of a considered and concerted business practice. Consequently, there has been a degree of self-deception on her part regarding the extent to which she was involved ...

'For the reasons I have given, this claim is dismissed.'

Justice Steyn said that a significant part of Rebekah's evidence 'was manifestly inconsistent with the contemporaneous documentary evidence, ... was evasive [or] implausible'. She also said it was likely that Caroline Watt 'undertook the direct act' of passing the information to the *Sun*.

'I have found that Ms Vardy was party to the disclosure to the *Sun* of the Marriage, Birthday, Halloween, Pyjamas, Car Crash, Gender Selection, Babysitting and Flooded Basement Posts.' She also said, 'The evidence ... clearly shows, in my view, that Ms Vardy knew of and condoned this behaviour, actively engaging in it by directing Ms Watt to the Private Instagram Account, sending her screenshots of Ms Rooney's posts, drawing attention to items of potential interest to the press, and answering additional queries raised by the press via Ms Watt.'

I was surprisingly quiet through all this, trying to take it all in, but with everyone chatting away, I wasn't watching the time. Consequently, my phone was pinging messages by the time the call was over. It was now past noon, but I hadn't gotten to phone Wayne or my mum and dad to tell them the news. The ruling had already gone public.

By the time Kai's photo shoot was finished, my family WhatsApp group had gone into overdrive. When I got home, Mum and Dad were already there, so excited and relieved – even more thrilled than me, if I'm honest. I was strangely numb. Happier that it was all over than anything else. So many times, over the past couple of years, I'd asked myself, *Coleen, why did you do that? Why did you put up that post? Look at what it's cost, look at what it's caused and all the grief it's bought on the family.* That day, I knew why I'd done it. I knew why I'd stuck to my guns and seen it through. I'd been betrayed and then lied to, and now everyone else knew that to be true. All the people who had doubted me or thought it was all just a load of stupid nonsense knew.

Before I knew it, my brothers had joined us at the house, and we all sat in the garden drinking champagne. It wasn't the sunniest of days, but the world seemed like a brighter place for sure. Meanwhile, I was getting messages from all over the place. My friend Danielle, who was at a wedding, sent a picture of her table at the reception, all raising a glass to me. Another group of friends had gone out for a celebratory drink in my honour, while others messaged to say how proud they were that I'd seen it through. It was quite overwhelming to think that my friends were all out there celebrating my good news, but at the same time, I knew I was in the right place. I was in my own home, in the garden with my family. I felt at peace for the first time in a long, long time.

The only thing missing was Wayne, who'd had to return to America for work. I'd have loved him to have been there with us that day.

The following morning, I woke up having slept in – bearing in mind that a sleep-in for me is 8 a.m. By then, it was all finally sinking in, so I decided to sit in bed and thank all the friends and family that had messaged me the day before. Eventually, I went downstairs, and there was a bunch of flowers on the kitchen counter.

'Who are the flowers off?' I said, knowing full well my mum would have opened the card and had a nose the minute she saw them.

'Oh, I don't know,' she said innocently.

'Oh, you've well opened that card,' I said.

'I haven't! It's addressed to you; they're your flowers.'

I knew she was lying, and as I opened it, my mum and sister-in-law Amy never took their eyes off me.

The card said, *Sorry, love Bekky.*

I took one look at the pair of them, and they burst out laughing. It was their way of helping me see the funny side, trying to make me laugh after all the stress and misery.

'I know you've done this; you've spelt the name wrong,' I said.

The rest of that morning, we just sat talking and relaxing. It felt like things were normal again. It was over – at least that part of it was.

Since it all went down, there's been a television drama-tisation recreating the court case, starring Michael Sheen as David Sherborne, and there's even been a play on in the West End about the trial. It's madness, really. When I first heard about the TV show, I wondered how they would do it. It wasn't a documentary; they weren't interview-ing Rebekah or following me around with a camera crew. Eventually, I found out that the script was put together from transcripts from the court. The writers had to be extremely careful to stick to what truly happened for legal reasons; they couldn't invent scenes or change the word-ing, so what people saw and heard on the screen was what happened. Well, not everything! During cutaway scenes from the courtroom, the actress Chanel Cresswell, who played me, was portrayed doing various bits and pieces in her home. While it was on, I got a sarky message from 'Brenda'. 'Since when have you baked bread or watered flowers in your garden with a watering can?'

Watching it was a very strange experience.

Chapter Twenty-Three

In 2022, when I took part in Wayne's documentary *Rooney* for Amazon, I stood in our kitchen with Wayne discussing the rough patches we've been through as a couple, Wayne's infidelity, and how hurt I've been at times. It wasn't easy, but the director asked us the question so we answered it. Our on-camera honesty surprised a few people.

'Oh, I didn't think you'd talk about all that,' someone said.

'Well, no one outside my close circle has ever asked me about it,' I said. 'I'm not embarrassed to talk about it. Everyone knows some of the details of what happened, but no one really asks me how I felt about it or what I went through.'

Of course, certain subjects are not easy to talk about or even think about, but that's one reason I wanted to write this book, so I could talk about it, tell my side of the story, and then move on. It just had to be the right time, when I was ready to do it.

I can't pretend my marriage to Wayne has been easy; it hasn't. There have been times when I thought he might be on the brink of a breakdown; in fact, he probably has broken down in his own silent way. There are other times when he's cried like a baby, and I've held him – times when things have gotten too much, and he's hit rock bottom.

Ultimately, it always comes back to the same thing, the pressure he's felt ever since he was a young boy. Over the years, people have criticised not only the things he's done but the way he looks, the way he talks, his performance on the pitch, and the decisions he's made for the good of his family. It's always there, bubbling just under the surface. It's all those voices that won't allow him to love or even like himself sometimes. And when the low points come, it's hard to know what to do apart from suggesting he talk to someone professional.

I know he finds that hard, though, speaking honestly, from the heart, about himself and his feelings. Wayne can be romantic and caring, and he certainly isn't afraid to show me that side of himself. He just can't seem to offer that love and care to himself.

Still, it all feels different now. Calmer, somehow, especially in this new house, which feels like it was a long time coming. Finding land that we were allowed to build on and then making sure all the planning permission was in place was a long and drawn-out process, and with the pandemic, the stop-start nature of the construction made it feel like it might go on forever.

Wayne's playing career is over now, too, so day-to-day

we're not in the glare of the spotlight. Although, saying that, I've probably given him a run for his money in that respect lately. We have a good life, though, and our beautiful boys are now at that wonderful stage where all four of them are into various sports and activities, both in and outside of school.

I'm lucky that I'm able to be there at sports days, fixtures and special events. I enjoy the experience of watching from the sidelines and cheering them on. It's one of the best things about being a mum.

It can be tricky, though, with them all being different ages. It's tough to find one place where they'll all be entertained. These days, I tend to do separate outings or trips in the summer holidays, taking each one of them out to a place of their choosing with their choice of friends. Sometimes it's a day, sometimes an overnight stay, but it's up to them what they do – within reason! That way, I get to spend quality time with them all separately, while they, in turn, appreciate that special time with me.

Whatever's going on, I do spend a lot of time in the car. That's my thing – I'm constantly in the bloody car.

When I was a kid, everyone was welcome in our house. My brothers and I always had our mates around, and the place was always full of noisy kids. Even as we got older, if I'd been on a night out with the girls, we'd invariably end up back at my mum's, rounding off the evening or having a nightcap.

I want that for my boys, I want them to feel that freedom, but it's a headache right now. If Kai brings a friend home, the little ones will all surround that friend; they all want to get in on the action. Then Kai will get moody, and there'll be a fight when he tells them to go away – it's bedlam. It's much easier if one of them has a mate over, and the rest go off on play dates to other friends' houses. Spread it all out, I say!

The mornings can also be an exercise in self-control too.

'Do you want to go and brush your teeth?' becomes 'Can you go and brush your teeth now, please?' becomes 'I've asked you twice, now can you go and brush your teeth?' becomes 'GET UPSTAIRS AND BRUSH YOUR TEETH NOW!' I can morph from bright and breezy to screaming banshee in a very short space of time. I love it, though. I wouldn't have it any other way.

I was approached about the possibility of making a documentary about the whole Wagatha saga by a number of production companies. At first, I wasn't sure I wanted to get involved, but the more I thought about everything, it made sense for me to tell my own story in my own words. I asked Paul to deal with all the negotiations, but I had one stipulation – no filming was to take place until the trial was over. I had enough on my plate preparing and being ready for court.

Still, with the trial over, I've had to think about what comes next. How am I going to manage life in the public eye, and is that something I even want?

Since I put out that now infamous post naming Rebekah, we've been inundated with offers for exclusives from TV stations and magazines worldwide – some very high-end. I could have jumped on it early, but I didn't want to rush into anything before all the facts were in place. Then, once Rebekah announced she was taking me to court, I couldn't say anything anyway. It might have got me into even deeper shit, or I might have screwed up my defence by giving too much away. Right now, I'm pleased I waited.

This book and upcoming Disney+ documentary give me the breathing space to tell things from my perspective. While the madness was happening throughout the trial, I never felt like people were hearing the entire story. It was just the juicy bits, the soundbites and the significant revelations. And then, of course, there were countless opinions that I had no voice to challenge.

'Why can't they just ring one another up and have it out,' the presenters on the daytime talk shows would say. 'Why is this news?'

Well, because you've made it news. You've made it entertainment, and yes, I totally get why. People love this shit! The truth is, this was never just some schoolyard cat-fight or a pair of WAGs tearing strips off one another. Something horrible happened to me, and I tried to stop it in the only way I knew how.

The documentary filming was an emotional experience. We shot a master interview that lasted two and a half days, which was quite hard going. Raking over it all again in that environment, with a camera on me, was intense. I can't say it was enjoyable, but it was undoubtedly cathartic – telling it all out loud with nobody in the opposite corner, disputing my version of events. It's been a long process; we did it over about ten months, but it's not been too intrusive. The team making it has worked around me and fitted in with our schedule. It's been managed well.

I've told my side of the story now, allowing people to come to their own conclusions. What I can say is that both my book and the documentary really do give the complete picture in a way that just isn't possible through other forms of media.

Rebekah has participated in a few interviews since it all went down, and that's fine. She said what she needed to say. Now I'm finally ready to tell things from my perspective. For me, it's about finishing the jigsaw and explaining how a betrayal of trust impacted my family and me and why I decided to do what I did. Once that's done, it's finished. I never need to do another interview about it. If someone asks me, I can say, 'Read the book,' or 'Watch the documentary.' That's my explanation, do with it what you will. It can be done with. I can move on.

And I do want to move on. In writing this book, it struck me that my life has had very distinct chapters. The last one was something I'd like to avoid repeating, but I'm now starting a new one. After a few years of upheaval and stress – moving to America and coming back to a legal fight – I feel like the clouds have lifted; things appear normal again. I lost myself for a while, but now I feel like Coleen again. My friends and family have told me that they feel it too. And yes, it's taken me a while to get my mojo back as far as entertaining goes, but I think I'm finally getting there. For so long, I felt I shouldn't be enjoying myself, and I didn't have the energy to try. Hopefully, now, I'll be back to my old self – party organiser extraordinaire.

So, what's the future for me? What do I want to do? I recently did a photo shoot for *Vogue* – talk about full circle. We shot some of the pictures at home and some on location around Liverpool. One of the shots was in front of the Liver Building, which felt nice, like coming home.

I was excited about doing a *Vogue* photo shoot at the house, but the day before the shoot, there was a little voice helping to keep me grounded. I noticed that someone had spilled something on the living room carpet, so, being the neat freak I am, I got down to clean the stain. While I was cleaning away, Kai was watching from the couch.

'What have you got on tomorrow?' he asked.

'Well, I've got a photo shoot, here in the house.'

'In the house, what's it for?' he said.

'It's for *Vogue*.'

'*Vogue*? You're messing, that's a big thing, isn't it?' he said. 'Is that why you're cleaning the carpet, 'cause *Vogue* are coming round to ours?'

'No, you cheeky get, I'm cleaning the carpet because someone's put a stain on it.'

So much has happened between the first *Vogue* shoot in 2005 and this new one. Not all of it's been good, some of it's been bloody awful, but so much of it has been amazing and beautiful. That's the stuff I want to hold on to and take forward, not the bad stuff. Let's leave that where it is, eh?

That first *Vogue* feature opened many doors for me; offers and opportunities I'd never have dreamed of came my way. Now I keep thinking – hoping – that it'll be the same again this time, that there'll be other opportunities, new dreams to fulfil. I'm certainly ready to step back into the world of work and tackle some new projects. It's one of the things I'm looking forward to most. I'm excited.

It's funny, I looked back at that 2005 *Vogue* interview recently, and as older and hopefully wiser as I am, I could still see so much of the woman I am today. I've learned a lot, but deep down, I've not changed all that much. Is that a good thing? Yeah. I think it is.

Acknowledgements

Mum, Dad, Joe, Anto, Amy, Carley & Kids.
I love our gang!!!
Thank you for always being there, loving me, helping me, especially with the kids and putting up with me.
I appreciate and love you all.
I am so lucky ♥

To all my and Wayne's family & friends (old & new)
I love you all, thank you for supporting me, checking in on me, laughing and crying with me.
You mean an awful lot to us.

Paul Stretford – it's been a long road for us both professionally and personally. Thank you for being by our side and for everything you do. We really appreciate it. A work relationship that has turned into a friendship.

Stephanie Lamon – I just love organisation and you are that!! Thank you for keeping me and my life in check, you are a massive help to us all.
Now my work sidekick . . . here's to many more of our laughs.

ACKNOWLEDGEMENTS

The team at Triple S Group – thank you for your continued support.

Myrna & Rodrigo
You are a massive part of our lives, thank you for all your help and being there for us all.

Jo
I know my kids are safe and happy when they are with you, which means a lot. Thank you.

Terry Ronald
It's been great spending time with you and chatting for hours on end. Thank you for your guidance with helping me tell my story – it will not be forgotten.

Paul Lunt, Jamie Hurworth, Adam Murphy & the team at Brabners, and David Sherborne & Ben Hamer at 5RB. Thank you for your hard work, dedication and support during the case and trial at the High Court.

My witnesses who stood alongside me in court: Claire, Harpreet, Joe, Mark, Paul, Penny, Rachel & Wayne – I can't thank you enough for being there for me during a difficult time in my life.

Dan Bunyard & the fantastic team at Penguin Random House – thank you for giving me the opportunity to tell my story.